W9-ARE-624

A12901 730321

4/08

SEE YOU
IN COURT

SEE YOU IN COURT

HOW THE RIGHT

MADE AMERICA

A LAWSUIT NATION

Thomas Geoghegan

THE NEW PRESS

NEW YORK
LONDON

Requests for permission to reproduce selections
from this book should be mailed to:
Permissions Department, The New Press, 38 Greene Street, New York, NY 10013.

Published in the United States by The New Press, New York, 2007
Distributed by W. W. Norton & Company, Inc., New York

LIBRARY ON CONGRESS CATALOGING-IN-PUBLICATION DATA

Geoghegan, Thomas, 1949–
See you in court : how the Right made America a lawsuit nation / Thomas Geoghegan.
 p. cm.
ISBN 978-1-59558-099-3 (hc.)
1. Justice, Administration of—United States. 2. Rule of law—United States.
3. Law reform—United States. 4. Trial practice—United States. I. Title.
KF384.G46 2007
347.73—dc22   2007010432

The New Press was established in 1990 as a not-for-profit alternative to the large, commercial publishing houses currently dominating the book publishing industry. The New Press operates in the public interest rather than for private gain, and is committed to publishing, in innovative ways, works of educational, cultural, and community value that are often deemed insufficiently profitable.

www.thenewpress.com

Composition by dix!
This book was set in Walbaum MT

Printed in the United States of America

2   4   6   8   10   9   7   5   3   1

CONTENTS

SEE YOU
IN COURT

PROLOGUE

A Warning at the Red Mass

Once, at a Red Mass a bishop from Rockford, Illinois, of all places, got me to thinking why the "Rule of Law" is in trouble here. But let me say with a blush what I was doing at a Red Mass in the first place. The big "Red Mass," or the Big Red One, is the one held in October in Washington, D.C., for lawyers and judges. The Red Mass kicks off a new Supreme Court term. By luck, one October, in Washington, I stumbled into it, the Washington, D.C., Red Mass, to which Supreme Court Justices like Antonin Scalia come.

That morning I saw a few Cardinals and at least two Justices, and my instinct, as a lawyer and a Catholic, was of course to fall on my knees to all of them, equally. Besides, they even share a few things, sartorially. They like to use a lot of red and black. They like to wear dresses. It's strange, to me, that when men rise to a certain star-chamber type of power, they tend to put on skirts.

I felt so powerless in a pair of pants.

The smaller of the two Cardinals gave the homily. He lauded us all: judges, lawyers, all of us, because we all love the Rule of Law. And the Church loves the Rule of Law: as the Roman Empire in its afterlife, it has always loved the Rule of

Law. For a few centuries many of the bishops, like Saint Augustine, did double duty as civil judges. They had no choice whenever a Dark Age came along. The Church is still around in part because it can step in for the legal profession when the State is going up in flames.

Anyway, that Sunday morning, I had a sense of solidarity with all those alpha males in velvet. "Yes, we lawyers run the world," I thought. "Look how we take care of others." Yes, at least on these ceremonial occasions, they may be rich or poor, it does not matter to us: we see them all as equal before the law. We do pro bono for the widow. We help the orphan. One might think, to go to a Red Mass or a bar luncheon, we spend half of our time in Legal Aid. I remember at my swearing-in, at a convention center, a state court judge in Illinois said, "As lawyers, throughout your lives, you will represent people from every walk of life, farmworkers, migrants, the disabled, the . . ." Then he quoted someone, I think Napoleon, on the Rule of Law, and then he swore us in, and for years I tried to be as compassionate as Napoleon. And now this morning, at this Red Mass in Washington, D.C., I felt the same nice glow I'd felt at my original swearing-in.

But the Red Mass is even better because I also get to see Scalia on his knees.

In Chicago where I live, we have a Red Mass of our own. And while it's not as good as the one in D.C., it's got its own appeal. We have a Cardinal—indeed, a very smart one. And while we don't get the U.S. Attorney General or the Supreme Court Justices, it's fine just to sit there with judges from the traffic courts.

Two years ago I heard a remarkable homily out here, and it was from the Bishop of Rockford, as I said at the start. Ah, Rockford, Illinois! As my brother said of it, "It's got all the disadvantages of living in a big city, with all the disadvantages of living in a small town." Our bulletin said that the bishop had lived in Rome, where he had studied canon law. What a comedown from the Vatican. After years of arguing over Aquinas and testing the carpaccio in the campagna, he'd ended up raising money in Rockford and getting pizza at the carryout.

But when he started his homily, I forgot about Rockford.

Not only was he smart, but in an eerie and unsettling way, he was uneasy about the Rule of Law. He began with a little joke, in Latin, involving the patron saint of lawyers, Saint Ivo: "Advocatus, et non latro, et mirando populo." "I would translate," he said, without a smile, "but I'm sure all of you know Latin."

I knew it of course: "A lawyer, and not a thief, and therefore a wonder to the people." I knew because my ninety-nine-year-old law partner, Leon Despres, knows Latin and had translated it for me many years ago.

And now the bishop began to talk even more darkly about the Rule of Law today. One feature of law, the bishop said, is that the people accept it as legitimate. That is the essence of the law. "And if the people do not accept a particular law as legitimate, it brings all the law into disrepute.

"And if all law is in disrepute," he concluded, "it can bring a type of anarchy." He seemed to suggest that people no longer felt they had consented to our legal system.

Was there any particular law to which the bishop was referring? He did not say.

At the breakfast that followed the Red Mass, I asked this of a man sitting next to me. He didn't know. "And did you get what he was saying to us in Latin?"

"No," he said.

And this man was a Jesuit. So I translated the Saint Ivo thing.

"Oh."

"Well, that was the least of it," I said. "Why did he keep saying that people have to accept the law as legitimate?"

"I wondered about that," said my friend.

"And if they don't accept a particular law as legitimate, it calls every other law into disrepute?"

Neither of us knew. But the bishop had made a big point—that we must give "consent." And he seemed to press on this: Are we lawyers so sure that people have given their consent to this legal system?

My friend and I were silent.

"Well," I said, "I'm sure he didn't mean it, but someone could say, 'Bishop, if that's so, then here's an argument from Church tradition, or Aquinas, why we shouldn't have a law banning abortion. If we do, and if people don't accept it as legitimate, it's going to call every other law into disrepute.' "

"I don't think he meant that," said the Jesuit, quietly.

Yes, I'm sure he didn't. But that's what opponents of the Church might well point out. If the Church got its ban on abortion, most people in this country would not regard it as legitimate. And if they openly break that law, does it not call every other law into disrepute?

But let's not get into that. It's the never-ending argument. Besides, I was interested in the bishop's hint that in some general way people in this country are not giving their consent to the laws we are imposing on them.

"Why should they?" I thought. "Fewer and fewer vote. Fewer give consent. We don't know really if people in this country accept the law as legitimate."

And we had just heard from a man who had once been at the Vatican. And to the Vatican's many secular scoffers I would say this: if a subject does not touch on faith or morals, the Vatican

can be dispassionate enough. Indeed, the Vatican can be a pretty cool observer. Because in the Vatican they know the world—and the world is a good judge. And if the world is uneasy these days about the Rule of Law in the United States, maybe we should give heed.

Don't people wonder what's going on here?

A few years ago I met a woman from Russia. She was in the United States on a short visit.

I said, "So how's America?"

"Oh, it's good. It's great." But then she lit her cigarette and dropped her voice. "Something is wrong here. What is it?"

"I don't know," I said. And then we began talking in normal voices.

And now it seems things have gotten even worse. Now we torture detainees. We start preemptive wars. "Oh well, we know that," many readers will say. But it's more than that. There's a sense of unease, of disengagement. Something is wrong. And whether it's a bishop posted to the Vatican or a Russian woman lighting a cigarette, I think most people in the world still want to believe: America, it's good. It's great. But something is wrong here. What is it?

Well, as a lawyer, I'd say this: more and more, people experience the law as arbitrary. I don't mean arbitrary as in unfair, but arbitrary, as in "unpredictable." I think here, especially, of the people I represent: middle-class or lower-income people. These changes all seem to happen without their consent. At first, I tried to put the argument in a pamphlet: *The Law in Shambles*. But I became obsessed: I felt I had to say more.

In the first chapters of this book I say much the same as I said in the pamphlet: contract law is being deregulated. Trust law is being deregulated. It is not just the New Deal that is being re-regulated, but even the law I learned in the first year of law school. But in later chapters I was itching to say more: oh, about class actions and releases and collection cases and all the new ways ordinary people get mistreated—not just as debtors but as creditors.

The more we "rationalize" the law to get out of the way of the market, the more irrational and arbitrary it seems to become. It may not seem that way to people at the top, to CEOs or those who show up at Red Masses, but more and more people now experience the law as arbitrary. Over the last thirty years, we have made big changes in the law. But to all these big changes, there has been no real consent.

To the contrary, people have dropped out. Fewer vote. Worse, fewer participate in making the rules, in their unions, in granges, in civic groups. People want more stability, but they keep getting less.

And one paradox is that the more we deregulate, the more we have to go to court—much more than fifty years ago. Today the working people I represent as a lawyer find themselves in court as plaintiffs in civil rights suits and as debtors in collection cases, but also as "creditors" in corporate bankruptcies. In nameless and uncounted ways, and often at the fringes, people are pulled in and pulled apart by what seem to be pure "business" cases.

As we deregulate and then pursue people in collection cases, and cut down class actions, more people at the bottom are in court, directly or indirectly. I don't mean just that the total number of lawsuits has gone up. Yet of course that number has gone up like a rocket. But what I mean here is that more people are being pulled in or pulled apart, directly or indirectly, by new types of litigation.

Let's put aside state court collection cases, rigged "private"

arbitration cases, and the like. Let's leave out the legally homeless, wandering around in the state courts and suing pro se, for
themselves. Let's leave out the rise in corporate bankruptcies
which have changed the lives of millions of working people.
Even in the federal courts, where it's very costly for ordinary
people to sue, there's been an explosion of cases. And in these
cases people find it's not just the law but the modern lawsuit
that is now "privatized" and "deregulated." To their shock,
they never see a judge. No one ever goes to trial. Clients are deposed outside of court or the presence of a judge, in private law
offices. They are insulted, scourged, and then returned to me,
to put ointment on their wounds.

And there is no one to protect them anymore: there is no
union to run the case, no National Labor Relations Board to
fight for them. People are turned loose to try to save themselves, to find their own lawyers, in a way they never were
thirty or forty years ago.

Getting rid of law does not end litigation. It often leads to
new types of litigation, especially the kind where people stalk
each other for revenge. Many get the urge to sue because some
business went after them. Of course, people go into court for
ridiculous things. They always have. But that's partly because
people don't know what the law is, so why not give it a shot? In
a deregulated economy that is addicted to making bets on
stock, on derivatives, on futures, I don't mind if the elite keep
piling into court. It's their taste for risk that helped to make
them rich. But it's harder for the poor or for people in the middle to deal with this uncertainty. They just experience the law
as more and more arbitrary.

And the more they do so, the more they withdraw from civic
life. We now get about 35 to 40 percent of eligible voters turning out in off-year Congressional elections, even "watershed"

elections like 1994 or 2006, which change the destiny of the country. It's not just the voting rate. People stop reading the paper or watching the news. They stop participating in any way in any civic life at all.

The Bishop of Rockford was on to something. So was the Russian woman lowering her voice.

Something is very wrong here. What is it?

CHAPTER 1

Do We Have Too Much Democracy?

A few years ago, *Newsweek* columnist Fareed Zakaria had a nifty op-ed argument, which he pumped up into a book, *The Future of Freedom: Illiberal Democracy at Home and Abroad.* Zakaria's point was this: in the Third World and in the United States, there is too much democracy and too little Rule of Law. Zakaria then tried to connect "illiberal" democracy in countries like Iran with a certain "illiberal" or excess of democracy in the United States.

Roll back democracy, he argued, and let's have more judges and lawyers. Let's have our elite make up more of the rules.

Now, it seems hard to believe that the United States, of all countries, suffers from too much democracy. In 2000 we elected a president who lost the popular vote. We have a Senate where forty Senators representing less than ten percent of the population can block any bill. We have a House in which most of the time less than a tenth of the seats are seriously contested. There is so little democracy that in a typical presidential election only half the country even bothers to vote—even less in off years, when the issue is merely control of the House and Senate. Often just a third of the people decide who will be Governor of a major state.

That's too much democracy?

Apparently, Zakaria wants even more elite rule, insulated from the mob. Here are his examples: the Federal Reserve Bank, the Pentagon, the U.S. Supreme Court. They work great! Take the Supreme Court: The Justices deliberate. They act reasonably. They can save us from the caprice of Congress. They can save us from the sense that the world is arbitrary and irrational.

This is an old Whig argument: it is the argument on behalf of rule by powdered wigs. For centuries, they have been saying that before there can be democracy, there needs to be the Rule of Law. And that means Magna Carta, the Domesday Book, Blackstone—the work of centuries. Let's not rush into Democracy! Democracy is arbitrary and irrational. Look at members of Congress: They grovel for PAC money. They have to play to the mob—or maybe even the Mob. Too much Democracy can undermine the Rule of Law.

Anyway, is Zakaria right? Do we have too much democracy? Maybe if there were fewer of us voting, we'd have more Rule of Law. I doubt it, but let's assume there would be more stability. Why is that good? Because we'd be more certain what our rights were. And in this respect Zakaria may be on to something. People in the United States might be happier if they knew what to expect, if they knew what their rights were. Maybe they'd stop experiencing the world as arbitrary and unpredictable. Or maybe, as a lawyer, *I'd* stop experiencing the world as arbitrary and unpredictable.

Yes, if that's all he wants, I think Zakaria is on to something. And the Bishop of Rockford is on to it, too. In Rockford, and all over, as we deregulate the labor laws, downsize even our corporate crown jewels like Ford and GM, cut back pensions and health insurance, people are experiencing the world as more and more arbitrary and unpredictable. Or at least that's how my clients seem to experience it.

But is Zakaria correct, that we have too much democracy?

Well, I admire Zakaria for writing his book, and maybe one day, if I ever try another piece of writing like this, I can give the man his due. But no, I don't think he's correct. I think he is terribly wrong. It's the *lack* of democracy in our country today that undermines the Rule of Law. People dropping out of civic life has had a negative, corroding effect on the law. The law is less stable, less predictable. So the world becomes less stable, less predictable. And as the world becomes less stable and predictable, more people drop out of civic life.

Why would anyone say we have too much democracy? In the 1996 presidential election, for the first time, over half of eligible voters didn't even vote! That's a cosmic kind of thing, isn't it? The nineteenth-century French historian François Guizot described the history of Europe as one in which more and more people take part in decisions. He found it hard to imagine the opposite—that is, the process going backward, with fewer and fewer choosing to take part in decisions.

True, one can claim that this reverse process is happening in other countries. Even in France and Germany, the voting rate has dropped somewhat. But why has it happened in such a big way in the United States?

Let me talk about three Big Facts. Around each of these facts I have tried, pretentiously, to write a separate book. The first Big Fact is the collapse of American unions. How did this happen? As I tried to explain (in *Which Side Are You On?*) it happened through the gradual loss of the right to join a union, freely and fairly, without being fired. Without that right, the

U.S. labor movement collapsed. In 1958, unions covered 34 percent of private-sector employees. Maybe more, say some historians. And in the North and Midwest, where the real economy was, the percentage was much, much higher, maybe 60 percent or more in some big cities. In 2005, labor is down to 7 or 8 percent of the private sector. Who could have guessed it back in the golden age of 1958?

In a sense, the flowering of the New Deal came years after Franklin Delano Roosevelt. By the right to bargain through unions, we came more than halfway to European-type welfare. It was a private-sector kind of socialism. Company by company, in a rocky, uneven way, more Americans got pensions, health care, and supplemental unemployment benefits. By the 1960s, in the steel and auto industry, workers were even getting European-type vacations, every four years, like a sabbatical. If it was not universal—if it was not "Europe" for all of us—it was "Europe" for more and more of us.

As in Europe, people became not just political citizens with the right to vote, but social citizens with the right to certain benefits. If I was a citizen, that meant I had rights. These rights, though legal, were not constitutional. They were contractual. But it did not seem to matter: the rights—to a pension, to health care, to vacations—would keep on spreading. They *felt* as if they were constitutional.

But they weren't. And they didn't keep on spreading. These rights—not the negative ones (for example, the right *not* to be detained), but the positive ones (for example, to pensions, health care, welfare)—began to disappear. The positive rights also that allow people to engage in "the pursuit of happiness" began to disappear.

Why? Labor unions collapsed. I wish there were another reason, because I'm a labor lawyer. And for a labor lawyer to blame it all on one Big Fact seems pretty self-absorbed. Okay, I'm sorry. And, indeed, I can say labor collapsed for more than one reason. There were several. The New Deal labor laws were pretty hollow: yes, people had a right to organize, but the 1935 Wagner Act, for example, has no sanctions against employers when they fire labor organizers. This began to matter in 1947, when the Taft-Hartley Act curbed labor's power to hit back through wildcat strikes, secondary boycotts of neutral employers, and mass picketing. When workers had to rely on "the law," there was not much law there after all. Another reason was the nationalization of the economy: thanks to such things as air-conditioning, the nonunion South and West opened up. In the 1960s and 1970s the United States became, at last, a truly national economy. This nationalization of the U.S. economy was at least as destructive as globalization is today, maybe more so. As employers moved into nonunion areas of the country, the unions found out how hard it was just to rely on the rickety Wagner Act to organize. Employers found out they could violate the Wagner Act, openly laugh at it, and nothing would happen. They could fire the pro-union firebrands or make illegal threats—and they wouldn't even be fined. The National Labor Relations Board would take years to hear these cases and could not even enforce its own orders, except by filing a new lawsuit of its own. By then, what would be the point? The drive to organize one or another particular employer would have ended years ago. The employers could run into court when the unions tried to strike. The workers had no right to go into court at all.

There were two asymmetrical legal systems: the employer's labor law, which worked—and the employee's labor law, which didn't.

So in the 1960s we entered an era of mass civil disobedience—not by civil rights marchers taking buses to the South, but by companies running from their unions in the North. Companies simply picked out pro-union workers and fired them, in blatant violation of the Wagner Act because the Wagner Act had no teeth. In the June 1983 *Harvard Law Review* Paul Weiler wrote that employers were firing at least one in twenty workers in the course of every contested organizing campaign. He based his estimate on final adjudicated cases: not just from the Carter NLRB but from the Reagan NLRB as well. As with any calculated purge, these companies went after working people who were the most "civic-minded," the leading citizens, the types who go to meetings.

Our worthiest citizens learned a terrible lesson: don't stick your neck out, don't worry about your neighbor, don't get involved. All these illegal firings had a paralyzing effect on the political life of this country, as it is lived out at the median income level and below.

And because employers have the "right" to engage in this kind of law breaking, all the other tactics to break unions are so much more effective. People can be brought in, held captive in one-on-one meetings or in large groups, and one by one, as they sweat, they can be threatened with pay cuts and loss of work. What can they do? "Look what happened to Smith!" Just one firing is enough. As Cornell University professor Kate Bronfenbrenner found, the culture itself is now so defeatist that only a minority of employers now have to engage in such firings. But whether it is a firing or any other illegal tactic, there is no way to hit back. The Wagner Act is like a prison in which working people are lost to the sight of the outside world. Lawyers can't help. There is no place to go but the NLRB, which has no power to do much of anything, even if it had the right appointees. I have often wondered about the shock, or the aftershock, of so many of these illegal firings. It's tempting to think of the employment law or discrimination suits, that rose sharply in the 1990s as a kind of payback—maybe a son or daughter who thinks, "I'll sue the bastard." And the abusive use of the deposition by the company—did that come out of the techniques of union busting? Now with the unions more or less gone, I often come across press releases from the Chamber of Commerce or the National Association of Manufacturers, proclaiming that "Our biggest problem is with lawyers." It may be true—since they sure don't have any problems with the unions they've destroyed.

But it's partly because they kept the unions out that employers today now face all these lawsuits. Indeed, employers should be grateful: this kind of litigation will not do what a union would. It will not raise wages. It will not put in a pension plan. It will not reduce a CEO's supersalary. Indeed, as I hope to explain below, this wave of payback litigation in tort-type civil rights cases may have the net effect of making the rich even richer.

At any rate, this is my first and favorite Big Fact: the loss of a legal right to put in a union. It is true that some unions have lost their nerve, even when they could win. Some unions try to organize outside the NLRB. But there is truly no way to organize outside the law generally—outside Taft-Hartley, for example, which prohibits much of what labor used to do routinely to organize in the 1930s and 1940s.

In no other developed country, at no other time in history, has there ever been such a steady increase of inequality as there is the United States today. "Oh, it's globalization," people say. But a global comparison rules out "globalization." Nothing has happened, even remotely on this scale, in France, Australia, Canada, Germany, Austria, Sweden, Japan, or Korea. Meanwhile, the

American GDP soars, productivity soars, yet incomes go down. But we have lost so much more than just income. Often there is:

- No pension
- No health insurance (or it's the kind with staggering $5,000 deductibles)
- No vacation (literally)
- No sick pay (in fact, you can't even call in sick)

So much for Big Fact No. 1. It is a measure of the loss of *social* citizenship.

Then there's Big Fact No. 2: the drop in the voting rate. This is a measure of the loss of our *political* citizenship. It's not just that fewer and fewer of us are still social citizens, with the social and economic rights that unions bring. It's not just that fewer of us have pensions, health care, or vacations (all that I blame on the collapse of labor). Even worse, more of us are resigning as political citizens. More of us feel we no longer have a stake in our country; we don't owe it a vote. In the 1996 presidential election we hit a new low, with by some estimates, less than half of the eligible citizens voting.

But then of course we had the uptick in voting in 2004. So do I take it all back? In the wake of the election, editorial after editorial read: "Voter apathy is dead!" "Mass turnout!" "Five-hour waits!" *Oh, come on.* It did go up—to 60 percent. But in part we got this higher percentage because we are getting better at calculating who's "eligible" to vote. That is, we are better at containing and subtracting ex-felons, the undocumented, and others from the baseline number of potential voters.

Besides, in 2004 we had billionaires spending billions, on both sides, to nag, harass, and literally pull people to the polls. It also helped that we had recently been through a major terrorist attack and were then in the middle of a losing foreign war. A better test of civic spirit is whether Americans vote more or less when no one is spending billions to pull them to the polls—for example, the 2006 primaries drew well under 16 percent of party voters.

Overall, we are now better-educated, with more college degrees. But we are well below the turnout of generally less-educated Americans in the 1960s and earlier decades. How is that progress, in Guizot's sense? "But other countries have seen declines." That's true, but these are much smaller. And in contrast to other countries, what is unique and disturbing about the United States is how many of the less-educated working people in our country are not even *allowed* to vote. They are not even counted in determining the percentages. The Sentencing Project estimates that over 4 million adult Americans are legally barred from voting because they are ex-felons or on parole or probation. In Florida there are over 600,000 ex-felons barred from voting, a number corresponding to one and a half percent of Florida's electoral votes. Add in 12 million Americans, hard-working taxpayers, who can't vote because they're here as undocumented workers. And even when they do become citizens, they vote at a rate 10 percent lower than even our apathetic native-born citizens.

In short, every year the United States excludes a higher percentage of the least educated, the poorest, and the most alienated from its voter base. Naturally, the turnout of those remaining appears to go up. But it's at least partly—not completely, but partly—a statistical illusion to say that voter turnout is increasing. Even so, the turnout for Bush versus Kerry in 2004 went up by only 3 percent or so. That's all that $4 *billion* in campaign spending could get. After all the beating on doors by Moveon.org and the awakening of the entire religious right, we got the equivalent of small change. And we did it in an election that was supposed to be as epochal as that of 1860, or at least was supposed to be a referendum on Iraq.

So why *did* people stop voting? There are many reasons, but one big one is, for men especially, the labor laws collapsed. People vote and vote, but they get nothing back—little or no pension, less and less health care—even as they go on working longer and longer hours.

"Why should I vote?" they say. People no longer sense there is a quid pro quo.

Worse, without labor unions, there are fewer institutions that "socialize" people, that is, tell them, "This is how you should vote, and why." Other institutions collapsed, too. There are no more farmer granges. There are no big city machines. But we could have saved the unions.

The more we de-unionize, the more people keep out of public life and the smaller and more volatile the electorate becomes. The republic is less stable. Over time, this means it drifts further to the right.

This is helped by the third Big Fact.

Big Fact No. 3 is the increase in prison, which has given rise to a class of noncitizen "untouchables." Since I got out of law school in 1975, the number of people in prison has increased by a multiple of seven. And we have more who wear ankle bracelets and are merely on probation.

Maybe I should include the undocumented, the 12 million, who are "illegal" in a way.

Of course they don't vote. But it's led to a whole rage against civic life. It's a much more radical withdrawal than merely not voting. And the rage gets into the popular culture, thanks to hip-hop and rap. It's cool to be disengaged. And this gets up to the dorm rooms of Harvard and Yale.

We can identify with the guarded or we can identify with the guards. That's a second evil: more and more of us are developing the moral character of guards.

And the more prison, the worse for public life. Our country has become an experiment in whether large numbers of "legal" and "illegal" people can live together. Instead of celebrating equality under the law, we are developing more of a Hindu sense of caste.

Once at a party a younger person (that is, someone under age fifty) asked me, "What *was* it like in the 1960s?" I decided to say the first thing that came into my head. "Well," I said, "no one was being executed." I might have added: even in Texas. Hardly anyone was in prison either, by our current standard. Later, I wondered what prompted me to say that instead of "Sgt. Pepper."

I was trying to tell him that it seemed possible then that we could let "captives go free," in Isaiah's sense. Now we lock them away.

I know a man, a reporter, who has to cover prisons as part of his beat. When he talks to a prisoner the first time, he asks, "Does anyone ever come to see you?"

"No," the prisoner says.

"It's always the answer," he said to me.

Of course, maybe the Bible says we should go down to see them. But even some of us who like hip-hop identify more with the guards.

By the way, how did we get millions of our fellow citizens in prisons? Answer: The labor laws collapsed.

All right, as a labor lawyer, I do have a single answer for everything. Yet even some labor economists admit as much.

Richard Freeman, a labor economist at Harvard, has made much of the shocking 30 percent drop in the hourly wage. It is a drop that happened just as the crime rate shot up in the 1970s. Freeman can only speculate if it led young men into crime. No, of course no one factor explains anything. But Freeman is not the only one to tie the rate of crime to the hourly wage. So did the famous economist Henry Thomas Buckle. The rate of crime, Buckle argued, is tied directly to the price of a loaf of bread.

But he would have said: It's the minimum wage. Were there other factors? Of course!

That's the academic if not politically correct answer. I know what to do when I see a question on an exam: "The prison rate went up: discuss factors, etc." Yes, it's also true that being a labor lawyer, I am blinkered. But it doesn't really count as thinking to "discuss factors," beginning with climate, demography, and so on.

The drop in the entry-level wage did come at or near the same time as the lockup that began in the 1970s. In turn, by "tightening up" the supply of labor, the continuing lockup of young males may have helped pull up the entry-level wage in the mid-1990s. By "taking criminals off the street," we made labor a bit scarcer. The entry-level wage went up; crime went down. That's a better reason why crime went down, inexplicably, in every major city, all at once, in the early to mid-1990s.

By 2006, after a long slow drop in the entry-level wage, it seemed that crime—street crime, violent crime—is starting to go up.

While each book I wrote had its own little Big Fact, there is one Big Fact that loops in and out of them all: unfairness. Most get less and less, even as the country gets more and more.

The Big Fact is not just the income inequality, but the sense of civil inequality that comes with it. And it's not a misperception before the law. As the income inequality gets worse, I have seen big changes in the legal system, or perhaps I should say "legal doctrine." Changes in the kind of law I was taught in law school. I think even bigger changes are still to come. We may still be "equal before the law." For now. Maybe. If we are here legally. But even if it's true for now, how much longer can it last? The rich will get richer. Even if they are undertaxed (and they are), they still pay the bulk of the taxes. In the future, they will pay even more. And why would they pay for a Rule of Law that applies equally to all of us?

Let me give a small example. Back at law school in 1974 I had to take "Corporations." I learned that directors had a fiduciary duty. They had to act with "prudence," "care," and "loyalty" to the corporation. They had to act in the best interests of the corporation.

Now this seems a starry-eyed left-wing kind of law.

But last year, a chancery court in Delaware rejected virtually half of what I learned in "Corporations." The court ruled that Disney directors could pay out a bonus of $140 million to a vice president they had decided to fire. That's $140 million, on top of his salary, after one year of work!

Let me give a sense of the old rule of law. In Germany, as I write, there is a criminal prosecution of a leading German banker, Josef Ackermann, for handing out a total of $56 million in benefits to a group of former executives. Ackermann's single biggest payout was $15 million.

The old rules that used to apply to people at the top no longer apply. And the rules that used to protect people at the median or below no longer apply either. Thanks in part to the collapse of the old law, the top 1 percent now take about a quarter of the increase in the U.S. national income. They leave less and less for the rest of us.

It seems harder to use a term like "us" to describe us as a country anymore. In an op-ed I read in late 2004, Robert Shiller, an economist at Yale, estimated that a few years ago, the bottom 40 percent of American families still received over 18 percent of all national income. Now it's under 14 percent, he wrote. Soon it may be under 10 percent!

If it drops under 10 percent, God help us; it will be truly hard to imagine all of us under a single Rule of Law. I know, we are numb to it. But even a small drop could have a devastating effect. It's not the income inequality, but the sense of unfairness and futility that is so destabilizing.

Whatever else it does, it weakens the moral character that we need for the rule of law. Yes, the rich are less responsible for the rest of us, or act with less restraint. But it's the middle class that worries me. There is good reason to think that as this inequality in the United States explodes, the middle class itself is becoming more corrupt.

Corrupt? Yes. Consider this single fact: It took ten years—almost all of the 1990s—for the median family income to get to the same level that it was, in real terms, in 1989. But in 1999, when we got to the same income level we had in 1989, the "median" family had to work six more weeks a year.

To keep from falling, the 1999 middle class had to work six more weeks a year for free. Not a few more hours—six more weeks! By the way, maybe it's worth pausing to say this: No wonder our GDP keeps shooting up, if the middle class is being forced to work for free.

But all this unpaid extra labor tends to undermine the Rule of Law.

Why? The economist John Maynard Keynes put it best: "Nothing corrupts a society more than to disconnect effort and reward." That's what did in the old Soviet Union: no matter how hard one worked, one could not get ahead of someone who did not work at all. And that is what is happening in the United States, too. Of course, in a certain way our country would seem the very opposite of the Soviet Union. Here, if people don't work, they're going to end up homeless. Then again, if they do work they may end up homeless, too.

That's the point. Like the USSR, we are slowly breaking the connection between effort and reward. And in terms of the Rule of Law, that's a dangerous thing to do. It's dangerous to push the middle class into questioning the fairness of the rules.

The danger is that people in the middle class will begin to see the world as arbitrary and unfair—unpredictable, a matter of luck, a chance of catastrophe around the corner. It does not matter if they work the extra hours. Over 40 percent of American families have less than $5,000 in savings. One bill, a hurricane out of the blue, can blow everything away.

So, quietly and to themselves, people at the median or below have to wonder, as the country becomes fabulously wealthy: Why play by the rules?

I may even understate the case. The disconnect between effort and reward is much greater than it seems. Some families lost income, though they worked harder. But they became wealthier. How? They made money off their homes. But this is not "effort." It's not even savings. It's just something that happened arbitrarily, to me, but not to many others. The moral is: Hard work doesn't pay.

Let's go back to my earlier example. I doubt many people did actually get back to the same 1989 level of income in 1999. Think of pensions. Fewer working people had pensions, though they worked longer. Or they had bigger administrative fees. Think of health insurance. Fewer people had it. Or they had bigger deductibles. They lost out, even with six more weeks of work. Perhaps our moral character can survive one decade of that kind of thing, but it keeps going.

Why is this so dangerous for the Rule of Law? It's simple. If we do not expect the world to be reasonable and fair, then sooner or later we do not demand or expect those qualities from the law, either. We get used to arbitrariness and unfairness. Sometimes we take a certain glee in it—at least when arbitrary things happen to others. Worse, as fewer of us vote, or even watch the news, we experience the legal system not just as arbitrary but as alien. It's something that is imposed on us. We did not consent to it. We didn't vote.

Worse, the more we drop out, the more arbitrary and unpredictable the Rule of Law becomes. The unions, political parties, and other institutions such as the liberal churches helped us shape a certain legal system. When they began to weaken, the law itself began to change. It became less rational and predictable. It is not just that people now *perceive* the law as less rational and predictable. It really is.

Maybe the country will survive it. Maybe the less rational and predictable the law becomes, the more people will go along. They will accept it up to a point, as in backward societies, because they will experience the Rule of Law in the same way they experience the world.

In what way is the Rule of Law becoming less rational and predictable? Let me list some big changes, to which, in any conscious or deliberate way, most of us did not agree.

CHAPTER 2

From Contract to Tort

How We Experience the Rule of Law at Work

In the nineteenth century the British historian H.S. Maine wrote that the movement from tradition to modernity was one from status to contract. In the late twentieth century, I'd say a big change has been the way we have moved from contract to tort.

For most working Americans, for the kind of people I represent, this accounts for the biggest change in the way the law now impacts their lives. In the 1950s and 1960s, up to 35 percent of workers, especially men, were covered by collective bargaining agreements. As a matter of contract, each worker could not be fired, except for just cause. If he were fired, his union would file a grievance and argue that "just cause" did not exist under the contract. If it was not resolved at the grievance step, a neutral arbitrator came in and decided the case in a cheap, informal way, often without a lawyer. By the way, these arbitrators were truly neutral, more so than many judges today. To get business, they had to prove they were neutral, since both union and employer had to agree to them. The remedies? Reinstatement. Back pay. The idea was that under a contract, a relationship would continue, in some way—if only between the employer and the union. In a certain sense, the contract was always reinstated.

Contract also permeated the nonunion world. In business back then, the cultural norm was: what the hourly worker got, the middle manager got. If it was not a contract as such, it was at least a contract-based norm of fairness.

Now, from what I can see day-to-day in my own practice, this world of contract is gone. Few workers—under 9 percent in the private sector—operate under any kind of labor contract. The rest work under a Rule of Law known as "employment at will." That means you can be fired for any reason. Or no reason. Or a bad reason—like the color of your tie. At any time. With no warning. No severance pay. Nothing. Once, in Berlin, I taught a seminar on U.S. labor law for some European law students. Before teaching the Wagner Act, I told them about "employment at will," kind of as an aside. I found, to my dismay, that in each subsequent class I'd have to explain "employment at will" all over again. For European kids, it was too hard to take in. Get fired for any reason? At all? The arbitrariness—the *unfairness* of it—was shocking. It was new to them.

While it may sound like old law, in a way it's new for us, too. Yes, we talk of employment at will as common law, as if it went back to King Arthur and his court. But in the United States, we are firing people as we never have before. It can be a cold-hearted corporate downsizing or a red-faced shouting one-on-one. In *The Disposable American* (2006), Louis Uchitelle argues that this trigger-happy way of firing was unknown in the 1950s or 1960s. Indeed, I'd go back further. For most of our history, we have lived in an agrarian nation. We farmed or we learned trades in small towns. The old America needed labor. Employees were scarce. One did not casually fire them. Then with the New Deal, we had union contracts to prevent arbitrary firing.

Until unions collapsed in the 1970s, the United States did not know "employment at will" in anything like its current, universal, and highly arbitrary form. In the last thirty years, there has been a loss of contract rights—to a job, a pension, or even health care—unlike that in any other developed country. It is really a new legal regime that many Americans experience as infuriating, without being able to express that fury in an appropriate way.

Some turn that fury inward, on themselves. For others, they can sue in tort.

I hardly need to tell an American the meaning of a "tort." We're the country of railroads, cars, medical malpractice, toxic waste: we're the country where people run over people. But for readers from Greenland, I will define it. In the common law, a tort is a wrongful act—other than a breach of contract or a breach of trust. It is a wrongful act that injures you, a slap on the wrist, a slip on the ice, for which (usually) you want someone to pay money damages.

A tort is a payoff for your pain. It's a howl from the roof of a building. It's a claim for a broken arm or an invasion of privacy.

I like the definition in my Random House dictionary: tort is everything that's left over after the law of contracts and the law of trusts.

The point is this: as we stripped people of their contracts at work, many of them began to fire back in tort.

Though we as a people lose the right to sue in contract, we have more chance to sue in tort. Since the collapse of unions, Americans have flooded the federal courts with civil rights type claims, analogous to claims in tort. The employee says, "OK, you took away my contract, we aren't equals, but you can't violate me as a person!" As labor, or contract, law waned, civil rights, or tort, law waxed. Indeed, this waxing and waning came right out of Congress. For over thirty years, unions begged Congress to fix the Wagner Act, to let Americans join unions freely, fairly—without being fired. In 1977 and 1993, the unions lost by small margins, thanks to filibusters in the U.S. Senate. But, perhaps as a consolation prize for denying the right to contract, Congress would then add another "new" civil right: for race, age, sex, handicap.

Sorry, no contract, which is what labor wanted. But here's another civil right claim—another right to sue in tort. There are so many such rights now, it's tricky even for us veteran lawyers to know which tort best applies in a given case. You come to me and say, "I've been fired." Here is just a short list of the laws I have to think about.

- The Civil Rights Act of 1964, as amended in 1991
- The Civil Rights Act of 1871
- The Age Discrimination in Employment Act of 1967
- The Employee Retirement and Income Security Act (ERISA) of 1974
- The Occupational Safety and Health Act (OSHA) of 1970
- The Family and Medical Leave Act of 1993
- The Waker Adjustment and Retraining Notification (WARN) Act of 1988
- The Americans with Disabilities Act

Are there more? Yes, indeed—other federal laws, perhaps the False Claims Act, may apply here. And each state has laws, "implied" causes of action, all of them torts, where we don't consider whether the firing was fair, but whether there was an evil motive.

Some may scoff. "How can you not know which law applies. It's easy!" Is it? I just saw an older woman chaplain fired at a hospital at the University of Chicago. For the same firing, she could have five legal claims. Go ahead, list them. And the best claim of all is one that is not even on this list.

(Write me, and I'll tell you what her "best" claim is.)

The one claim they don't have is contract, a simple right to do the job and be treated fairly. And this is enraging to people, since the companies hand out "handbooks" that look like contracts and sound like contracts and have pages and pages of "rules." But there is a disclaimer: "This is not a contract." Here are your rights as an employee, but on page 100 it says: "Nothing herein is enforceable." *Warning: This is not a contract.*

Is there any other country that gives out "contracts" of over ninety pages, with no rights in them? I'll bet that at Enron, in the final days, they were longer, and they came in vellum binding.

But legally these big books are as worthless as the constitution of a Soviet republic. If anything, these paper constitutions just enrage people even more. "You mean nothing in this whole thing is enforceable?"

No.

When people are treated like suckers, no wonder they're in court.

This is our brave new world—not of labor law but of employment law. Not of contract but of tort law. In vaudeville or saloons, we think of the old tort as payoff. I'm in an auto accident. I have whiplash. Pay me! See, I'm limping! But the new tort, the employment tort, is not so much payoff: it's payback. Usually, people lose, but that doesn't matter. A big part of it is revenge. "At least we forced the bastard into court."

Even if they lose, even if they are acting pro se, people can sometimes force the employer to pay a staggering sum. In some of our federal courts, at least on the civil side, this new tort law is either the biggest or the most exasperating part of the civil docket for many judges. A magistrate judge recently told me that 40 percent of all the civil cases are now "employment cases."

I doubt it's *really* that high, but it may feel like it is. In 2000, the Bureau of Justice Statistics did a rare count of the filings of civil rights cases, just in federal courts only. (By the way, any count like this is rare; it's a shock to find out no one collects this kind of data.) From 1990 to 1998, the filings of civil rights cases in employment—just in civil rights, like race or sex— roughly tripled. By contrast, in civil rights cases for voting or welfare, the number dropped. One big reason for this increase was the passage of the Civil Rights Act of 1991, which beefed up rights to punitive damages and legal fees in race or sex cases. I'm sure another big reason was all the corporate downsizing of the 1990s: this was the era of Jack Welch and Chainsaw Al Dunlap.

But I hesitate to cite this study, because the real number of these cases was actually greater. How many were class actions? How many had four or five plaintiffs? I know I usually file with a group, even if it is not a class action.

Perhaps no one does the count because the counts tell us so little. A lawyer can have two hundred cases and handle them in a collection court in an afternoon. Another case, a single case, just one, can consume ten lawyers for over ten years. This week, to take a case at random, I became a co-counsel in a suit against a drug company. The original lawyer started with one woman, a top salesperson. The drug company replaced her with an ex-college cheerleader, a blond bunny who could lure the doctors into the lobby and giggle and say, "Would you like to see our pills?" But usually it's a pattern. In fact, other people lost jobs to bunnies. The drug industry is turning into a version of

Hooter's. Soon we may have a class: I'd say we need forty. It's common.

But that's just "one case."

It's the nature of these cases that you pick up others as you go along. My friend S told me the other night that she started with one woman—"You know, these perfume ladies in the department stores"—who was paid not as an employee but an independent contractor. Now S has a class of six thousand women. But sometimes there is no need to certify a class, so in the end, this counts as one case. But is it? Why count that case as statistically equal to a suit by a homeless vet, pro se, who's wandering around with aural hallucinations?

To me as a working lawyer it feels as if the number of civil rights cases has more than just "tripled." Even a suit for one person feels as if it were a class action. It is often just as much work as suing for 10,000 people in a class; we still have to prove a kind of "group" or "class-wide" discrimination, even if the suit is only for poor Ms. Smith or Mr. Jones. In fact it's harder than a class action since it's easier to pick off or explain away one person. "Oh, Ms. Smith is a lush, didn't you know?" But here's a puzzle: Why did the magistrate judge say "40 percent" when in 1998 there were 250,000 civil cases and only 42,000 were suits for "civil rights"? Ah, the answer is that she said 40 percent were "employment" cases. She means not just obvious civil rights cases (age, race, sex) but other types of illegal discharges, or cases about lost benefits. Plus, they often get state law employment claims. One judge calls them "the domestic relations docket of the federal courts." That's a bit cruel, but at any rate these are "intent-type" torts, or cases not about objective or external behavior but about what is lurking in the human heart.

At any rate, the magistrate judge was probably thinking of

all these new types of torts, not just the civil rights cases, but the ones that can arise under ERISA, or the Family and Medical Leave Act, or other laws. And there has been a similar or even bigger rise in state-law employment claims.

For Illinois, a cautious state, I could list a dozen new types of torts—suits for people who get fired for filing worker compensation claims. These are things that unions used to stop, but now there are no unions, so they are spilling into the courts. Here, alas, there are no numbers, nationally. Each state is so peculiar, too. The National Center of State Courts does not even count these cases as torts. To the NCSC, operating in the legal Stone Age, a tort is still a car crash.

But all these new worker claims are tort cases all right: about personal injury, except much more focused on feeling and subjectivity. And the suit often ratchets up the rage. People scream over something for years that a union business agent used to handle in a single afternoon.

In some ways, being fired is not as bad a thing as it was fifty years ago. I try to tell my clients, "Everyone gets fired." I told a friend in the arts world the other day, "Look, in the arts world, as I understand it, you're supposed to be fired. If you aren't fired at some point, it means you aren't competent. I was delighted to cheer her up. But to be fired is much more life-threatening than it was forty years ago. For example, having health insurance now is such a life-or-death matter. Lose your job and you lose your insurance.

"They're trying to kill me!"

Let me sum up, if I can, why it's so bad to go from labor contract to tort.

First, all the parties end up feeling violated. Unlike contract, the tort case is not so much about objective fact or "external" conduct, but about subjective intent or "inner" state of mind.

What the plaintiff must do is not just suggest, but "prove" that the employer tried to harm him for a specific evil reason. The point of the case is not to an "objective" or "external" act, as in the old labor contract case, but to find the "subjective" or "interior" intent—in a sense, to peer into the human heart.

And this unlawful motive or evil intent is harder to prove— we seem to argue in every case how much "evil" there has to be. Just recently, on appeal, our firm had a Title VII case on behalf of a group of black forensic scientists, chemists working in crime labs. The black chemists working in the city labs did *much* more work and had more years of service than the suburban, downstate whites who ran the department, but they were paid much less than their white equivalents. It should have been easy: over in a month.

But instead of a nice old arbitrator from a law school, we get a jury—and they're white. Since they're white, they can't believe it's "only" about race. Weren't there other motives here?

Sure, it's not *all* race. For example, suburban people don't like city people. Republicans don't like Democrats. There might have been other reasons, right? So the issue for the appellate court is this: Does race have to be "the" factor? Or only "a" factor? Okay, that's clear—after forty years of litigation, it's now settled that race need not be the "only" factor.

Yet it seems that we have to argue it all over in every case.

Even if it is only "a" factor, how much of "a" factor does it have to be? Does it have to be a *controlling* factor? Or only, as some say, a *catalytic* factor, as the judge declared in our case? Or does it only have to be a *substantial* factor? We say, not catalytic but only substantial. Do you agree? Here's the next issue: even if race is a factor, and even if a single factor is enough, can the employer still win by showing he'd have done the same thing based on a factor that he didn't consider at all?

Confused? So are all the rest of us. After forty years, and forty thousand case opinions, and repeated attempts by the Supreme Court to clarify, we were on appeal. Every time there is a case, it's "settled." Then in the next case it has to be settled again.

By the way, we lost our appeal for the black scientists. I mean, we won technically. The court found that we were right and the trial judge—a very liberal judge, by the way—was wrong on the race instruction. But the court denied the appeal anyway. It decided, in effect: "Yes, there were big legal mistakes, but they didn't matter."

Why? The jury was white. The plaintiffs were black. The Court of Appeals could have said to us, "Do we have to draw you a picture? It's over. You lost." In the world of federal civil litigation, it is rare enough that a case ever goes to trial. No one I know has ever gotten *two* of them.

By the way, according to the Bureau of Justice study, in civil rights cases, when plaintiffs go before a jury, they win only one out of three times.

But didn't the Court of Appeals at least clarify the law? No.

As I write, in courts all over the country, lawyers are litigating this again, as if it's for the first time, though both sides cite thousands of cases. At the end, the jury will still come back with a question. "How much of a factor?" A judge will think up a new test, such as "It has to be a *crucial* factor," and someone's on appeal, screaming, "That's not the law."

At the end of the case, I was embarrassed—for myself, for the jury, for all of us. Our clients were scientists. Quiet people. Shy. They were just being paid $2,000 or $3,000 less a year than their white counterparts. It should have been a contract case. We shouldn't have had to drag race into it—in a way, because it *was* a race case. That's why contract is better.

But because it was race, and motive, and intent, everyone felt violated. Our clients did. So did their bosses. So did I.

Second, unlike contract, the new tort law is expensive. Contract is simple. Tort is labyrinthine. The old arbitrations were cheap. There was no pretrial discovery. No big costs. It was done in a day.

Win or lose, I'd go home at night: "We're done."

Our firm had a flat fee for arbitration: $2,500. Now, in a tort case, my bill could be $150,000.

Am I asking too much?

Believe me, I deserve it because unlike the old contract cases, it's not "done in a day." It could take four or five years. I have two file drawers of motions to dismiss, summary judgment motions, twenty-five-page briefs, and two volumes of exhibits, which take five hours for our paralegal to scan. Now the fired employee has to come up with big money—$5,000, $10,000—and that's just for costs (the court reporter, depositions, photocopying).

Then we get to fees. Each side blames the other for "overlitigating." I blame the management firms, of course. For example, a judge often sees the same motion over and over. In several cases I've been in, the other side files a motion to dismiss (denied). Then it files the same motion but tweaked a little (denied again). Then it files a motion for summary judgment (denied), and on and on. Sometimes, the briefs can be half a foot high or so. And it's not one motion one time, as in the old days, but two or three of these in a case. No one wants a trial!

Meanwhile, there are depositions. As the companies become global, so does the discovery: for a case involving workers at a factory in Kankakee, Illinois, we have had to depose managers in Philadelphia, San Francisco, and Australia (by telephone).

In such cases, for a legal fee, our firm soon has a cash claim far bigger than any single client's! There's no union to pay—which might restrain us. So instead of one contract case, there are two: *Client v. Company* and *Plaintiff Lawyer v. Company*.

Plaintiff lawyers feel like we're victims of a tort—the front line when the other side wants to engage in slash and burn.

The old system? A union contract claim could cost between $6,000 and $15,000. That would be the total, all of it, including the fee of a nice old New Deal liberal serving as our arbitrator.

But the costlier the cases are, the deadlier they are. It's not just my fee, but their fee. If I'm at $150,000, the other side is paying out $350,000. And that brings me to the big difference.

Third, it's scorched-earth litigation. Or it's much more likely to be than in the old contract arbitration. For one thing, as I noted already, there was no discovery in the old contract type cases between unions and employers. In tort, the big thing is pretrial discovery; indeed, the cases never go to trial. And because there's no judge or kindly pipe-smoking arbitrator present, the questioning is meaner. The cases are meaner. In discovery, I can force you to tell me everything: what is in your secret heart, not to mention what's in your tax returns.

It's hard to exaggerate how big a change this is. Everyone in the case has to strip themselves, in a sense, take off their clothes, far more now than was the case when I started out in law school. Look at what Paula Jones's lawyers did to Bill Clinton—and he was a sitting president! What makes the new "American-style" tort law so bitter, so cruel and unrestrained, is discovery, with no judge around and with each side on a rampage to swing at the other's head.

Over what? Intent, motive. A "bad" state of mind. That gives a legal rationale to harass and destroy, in a litigation that is disconnected from whether the employee was treated fairly.

Obviously, it is terrible for the employer, and he or she is often right to complain. After all, most employers do not engage in "hate" crime, or at least feel they haven't. At worst, they really have mixed motives. But employers are responsible for doing away with the older, cheaper system. They discovered early on that the broader the discovery right, the bigger the employer's advantage. It was management lawyers who first showed us, the plaintiff lawyers, how to torture people in a deposition!

And with the new tort, there is no need to hold back on slash-and-burn. In the old contract arbitration, the goal was to reinstate—to put the employee back. The old union contract cases would try to restore community: if both employer and employee had to live together again, like a married couple, it made no sense to slash-and-burn. Let's be nice. But in the tort system, nobody is going back. Never happens. Not after the cost. Not after the $250,000 a company may pay its law firm. No way.

This is the legal system in post-union America. It forces us to cast legal issues in the most subjectively explosive way, as racism or sexism, because employers wanted to abandon the old system of "just cause." Do I regret becoming part of it? Yes. Are my clients often full of hatred? Yes. That's some of the blowback for busting unions. There is no union to restrain people, to put a hand on the shoulder and say, "Easy there, son. Don't throw that punch." Now no hold is barred. And that's true of management, too. After all, they aren't going to see this employee again.

So the irrational element is much greater. And, one may wonder, how often do employees win these cases? Outright, it's not often. Indeed, the idea is not to win outright. Look what happens with a jury in civil rights cases: you win only one out of three. Besides, more judges are conservative, Republican: they like to toss these cases.

Also, big business is much bigger than it was forty years ago. They can crush you. It seems hopeless. You can't win.

So why do people sue?

First, the companies are breaking these laws. Let's not forget that. But second, it's a kind of asymmetrical warfare. The little guy can force the company to settle just by not being knocked out. A few years ago I got a court appointment to represent a carpenter who originally had filed pro se. He was black, quite a good carpenter, apparently, and very bright.

Over the years he had filed two or more pro se suits, and joined with other black carpenters who had been shut out of projects. Yes, he was pro se, but he knew how to draft a complaint, and he even figured out how to keep his case from being dismissed. They might be able to jerk him around down at the convention center, but he had found out where his corporate bosses were vulnerable.

He could make them pay to get big fancy law firms to go after him in court. All he had to do was run around the ring and duck and weave, and the legal bill for the company would keep going up. He fired me, by the way. Why? "I want you to make this into a class action," he said. He wanted me to run around the ring too! I didn't have the time or money, or the taste for guerrilla law like this.

"No," I said. "You're getting me for free. I'm not going to file a class action."

Bang: I was gone. "You're fired." But he knew what he was doing. He probably could have taught me lessons in how to inflict damage on the other side.

My point is that this tort-type legal system, which replaces contract law, is a system that feeds on unpredictability and rage. Even if a plaintiff can't win, there's still a good chance that he can drive the other side nuts. A white-hot, subjective, tort-based law has replaced a cooler, more rational, contract-based law, which was modest and cheap and, best of all, kept us from peering destructively into one another's hearts.

CHAPTER 3

From the Law of Trusts to the Collection Courts

How the Charities Came to Prey on Beneficiaries

Perhaps a bigger change in the law, at least in my lifetime, has been the abandonment of trust law, the law governing charitable institutions. Today the "charities" that are set up to take care of us instead try to hunt us down. They sue the people they are supposed to help. Charitable hospitals give no charity—they sue the uninsured. Private colleges purport to be charities, but they drive students into bankruptcy. Big companies fight to be the sole fiduciaries of pension or health care plans, and pay themselves big salaries, but then with no warning, they decide to dump the plans. Oh, how I miss the law of trusts. Of course, I do labor law, but most of my practice has really been in the law of trusts: a kind of fiduciary law. It's what I argue in most of my cases. My clients are often working people who have lost pensions or health care. Usually a trustee has cast them away. It does me no good to argue that they have a duty of care. But if there is one legal doctrine that the law and economics movement has wrecked, it's the principle that we owe any charity to each other.

Hospitals, schools, and other charities don't give out charity even when they get a massive tax exemption for it.

Yes, the existence of the tax-exempt charity has allowed capital to gush into hospitals and universities. It's where the jobs are. It's where unions try to organize. MBAs now go into charity. It must be in business school where they learn to squeeze the poor, the elderly, the uninsured, for everything they can.

But that's not the worst.

Yes, even more than contract law, I miss the law of trusts! Back in law school, it was the law of charity that appealed to my tender side; maybe I had an inner flower child. But this body of law that had lasted from the Tudors up to Gerald Ford blew up when the labor movement collapsed.

Let's go back to 1975, when I had just got out of school.

In 1975, most working Americans were participants in various charitable trusts, via pensions and health funds. Now, for most people, these generous trusts are gone. This is a shock to people: there is no longer a trustee or fiduciary to take care of them. And here too, this big change in the law of trusts came out of labor's collapse.

I like to repeat this, because there is such a taboo against saying it.

Thanks to labor, we had come to have a nation of charitable trusts, that is, pension funds subject to the law of trusts. Often these were big multi-employer plans. They had something called "defined benefits," which meant that you got that big pension—that fixed sum of, say, $2,500 a month—even if the Dow dropped from 10,000 to 10. It wasn't your problem. Now if we have anything, we just have 401(k)s. That's a voluntary savings account. The boss does not save, as in the old system. You and I save.

We Americans are famous for saving, right? Result: no one has a pension. Of course I exaggerate, but not by much—even some of my friends who make over $100,000 have yet to start saving. But that's why we're Americans.

When we were all part of these legal charities, our trustees did the saving for us. They collected money from our bosses. Indeed, the bosses were the trustees: they held the money in trust for us. We the people couldn't get it, even to send our kids to college. We were the "beneficiaries." We had trustees, not just to save, but to save us from ourselves. It is a weird thing to say, but they had a legal duty to love us. Under the Employee Retirement Income Security Act, or ERISA, the trustees had, and still have duties, in the law, to exercise "prudence," "diligence," "care," and "loyalty." No, I'm not joking: these words are in the law. They had a duty to take care of us, in the same way they might take care of themselves. And so thanks to ERISA, a certain kind of love is law. They passed ERISA as I was about to come out of law school. Oh, the older lawyers told me then, this law will change our lives. It was a big deal. Some lawyers thought it might be even bigger than Social Security.

ERISA would spread the law of trusts to everyone. At least to everyone in those big plans that had defined benefits, as were typical of the time. How many were in such plans? Over half the workforce. So half of us now came under the care of guardians, or trustees. We could work till old age and know that someone would take care of us.

Now, years later, it turns out no one will be taking care of us.

When labor collapsed, employers stopped offering pensions—at least not the defined-benefit kind. That's the kind for which the employer, not the employee, has to save. But with this wonderful ERISA, how could the employer just stop giving a pension? Well, the law never said the employer had to *give* a pension. Once the pressure of dealing with a union vanished, employers either stopped offering any pension, or pushed people into 401(k)s or other similar "defined-contribution" arrangements.

And as people found out, when they landed in the 401(k)s— baby, they were on their own. The employer might, or might not, match their savings.

In a country where savings are less than zero, the concept of a 401(k) plan—whereby most of us, house-poor and broke, would voluntarily fund our own pensions—is fantastical. And soon, the defined-benefit pension will be gone. Except for a few cops and teachers. And for the rest of us? Teresa Ghilarducci, a labor economist at Notre Dame, estimated that, in 2000, at the height of the economic boom, the average 401(k) individual plan had no more than $24,000—the *average*. This included the top fifth of wage earners, who stash away millions. Indeed the 401(k) plan is an engine of inequality. People at the top build up their own, by taking it from the people below. I mean this literally. I was recently visited by a 401(k) consultant, who asked me, as he asks other employers, if I might want to "restructure" our firm's 401(k), to "appropriately reward" the "high-end earners." In other words, since the firm contributes to the 401(k)s, we should take it from the secretaries and give it to ourselves. He had closed the door of my office.

Why not? Steal it from her. No one would know.

Well, I won't say what I did. But whatever it was, no one would find out. The trustee, the old-fashioned trustee of the big ERISA plans, is gone. No one is there to stop people like me from bleeding my secretary's tiny account without her ever knowing. So, little people, beware. But it's more than just the risk that I may be "restructuring." The investment companies and banks that run these little savings accounts often cheat people, one by one, in nickel-and-dime ways. Because there is no real trustee around, the companies pile on fees and charges for handling the accounts, so any gain that poor secretary makes in the market is wiped out by a higher, usually hidden, fee. It's terrible. A friend of mine, John Wasik, a financial columnist, has been the pioneer in showing the way people are ripped off. Why don't we lawyers bring suits? Because the cheating is too small, microscopic, and hard for us to detect.

For one thing, employers aren't there to stop it. In 1988, about 90 percent of U.S. employers paid all the administrative costs of the 401(k)s: the fees, and charges. Now only 25 percent do.

Keep in mind, most people are putting in about $500 a year. Whoosh, with a fee or charge or two, people have actually lost money.

In this new world of little accounts, there are no fiduciaries—though they may say so on the bank cards or on our accounts. In truth, there is no one to save for us. There is no one to guard against the piling up of little fees.

So what happens? Without grasping what is going on, many people get less of a pension year by year. Restructuring. Hidden fees. Of course, if they turned it all over to Enron or World Com, they ended up with little or nothing at all. Because, unlike the old defined-benefit plans, 401(k)s aren't insured by the government.

In some 401(k)s, the employer matches what you or I save. But why bother? With no unions, the only reason the employer may set up a 401(k) is for tax reasons. And as the Bush administration keeps slashing taxes, there is less cause for the employer to match anything at all.

But here's what really makes it seem arbitrary. The employer can stop a pension plan, or a matching 401(k), or even our health insurance, without notice.

In one case in our office now, we are suing the directors of Outboard Marine Corporation (OMC). We allege that they cut off the health insurance of 6,000 people, with notice of eight days. Eight! Remember, these men are fiduciaries.

Eight days.

Yes, when they did it, OMC was in Chapter 11, bankruptcy proceedings. Still, OMC had literally millions in assets. They could have given our clients a decent notice. How did it hurt? We had 6,000 people who could have formed their own group for health insurance purposes. Much better than paying one by one. But we needed time so we could set it up and roll over our clients' coverage. For God's sake! Some people were about to go in for surgery. Others, chemotherapy. Couldn't they give us more than eight days? But with no notice, we didn't have a chance. I still have dreams about the daylong hearing we had in court, when the judge approved the cutoff of our insurance. All day, lawyer after lawyer for OMC or for the banks or for the other secured creditors stepped up to the judge and said:

"Your Honor, nobody likes to do this."

We asked for one hundred and twenty days. No. Ninety days. No. Sixty days? No. Finally, like Lot groveling before God, except without any hope, we asked for thirty days. No.

No. No. NO.

And more lawyers stepped up. Some I see at Democratic fund-raisers. "Your Honor, nobody likes to do this."

Or: "Judge, nobody likes to do this."

Or: "Of course, Your Honor, none of us likes to do this."

And the more they said it, the more I thought, *They certainly love to say it.* And I had the awful feeling that I often get at the end of the hearing: *They're going to come over and shake my hand.*

I usually warn co-counsel: "Get ready. When we lose they're going to come over and shake your hand." I worry that one of the younger lawyers might throw a punch.

Just kidding. Lawyers like us never throw a punch.

Later we brought a suit against some of these "fiduciaries." The District Court and the Court of Appeals have made it clear: they can terminate anything—a pension, health insurance—without even five minutes' notice. So part of the collapse of the old trust law is not just that they can do it, but that they can do it in a way that keeps people wondering, minute to minute, if they have any coverage at all.

But it can be worse than losing a pension or health insurance. More and more companies just spin off old units, and set up new ones, in order to bring in younger workers whose insurance costs are less. As I write this, I know of at least two big drug companies that are alleged to be doing so. In 2004, a group of workers here sued a company I will call Big Pharma I for this very thing. About this time, we met with about two hundred workers at another big drug company, who had more or less the same fate. The second company, which I will call Big Pharma II, had laid off over 400 workers and the manager told them there was no real hope they would be called back. Then, after the older workers took severance and resigned and signed releases, Big Pharma II started it up again, but now with the younger workers. Why? Our clients think it was to bring in a younger workforce that will cost Big Pharma II $11 an hour, instead of $20 to $22.

So people, in their working lives, experience the world as more arbitrary, more unpredictable. At Big Pharma II, there is no defined benefit. In some companies, there is no matching

401(k), and if there is, the little people who are in them are often hit with hidden administrative fees.

And of course, there's no health insurance.

Even if there is, it's often cut off with no notice. The old law of trusts is dead.

I'm afraid it gets even worse. Now the trustees, the guardians, often pick out the weakest of us, the poor, the uninsured, and sue them. I mean our charitable institutions: hospitals and universities. They get huge tax exemptions because they are so-called charities. They pay no property tax. They have tax-exempt bonds. (In effect, by exempting them from taxes, the legislature appropriates money to them.) Why? To help the poor and uninsured. Unless, of course, they end up in the emergency room, in which case these charities charge them two to three times what they charge insured patients, covered by Humana or Blue Cross. And when the uninsured cannot pay, the charities come after them in court. Their collection lawyers fill the courtrooms. They phone immigrants late at night. "How are you going to pay?" They go out and garnish people's wages. Then they try to destroy people's credit. Sometimes, as reported of late in the *Wall Street Journal*, they may even put them into jail.

And these hospitals are charities. They are set up *exclusively* for charitable purposes. How much charity do they provide? I used to think it was about 2 or 3 percent of patient revenue.

I was wrong. In a big legal challenge to one hospital out here, it was 0.7 percent.

Oh, but so many charitable hospitals in the inner city have closed! That's right—so they can open up in the suburbs, often the wealthiest ones. Then they don't have to deal with any poor people at all.

Besides, are they losing money? Do we know? Everything is off the books. Enron is a model of transparency compared to the typical charitable hospital holding company. They file no tax returns. There is no Securities and Exchange Commission to watch them. The IRS does not audit them or even bother to see if they perform charity.

The MBAs say that these charities are always broke—but somehow, they keep on getting bigger. The hospital expands. The doctor buildings next door get bigger. And they get some of their money by going to court.

Indeed, these new voracious "charities" are partly responsible for our litigation mess. When critics on the Right speak of The Legal Crisis in America, they mean, of course, the trial lawyers, people like John Edwards, filing suits against hospitals. The crisis was the subject of a *Newsweek* cover story, "Lawsuit Hell" (December 16, 2003). In that issue *Newsweek* gave big play to a lawyer, Philip Howard, author of *The Death of Common Sense* (1995). Howard is a partner at Covington & Burling. His argument in this best-selling book is that there is "too much law," and lawyers and lawsuits are ruining the nation.

Yes, of course, patients sue hospitals without restraint, for everything they can get. I find it appalling. But who started this war? Hospitals and doctors sue their patients far more than their patients sue them. If we simply count up filings, the real litigation hell is the explosion of suits by hospitals and doctors going after patients. In Chicago, many law firms exist just to chase patients: not only to collect bills, but to garnish wages and attach bank accounts—and of course, if need be, to press them into bankruptcy.

Fine, since you don't believe me, let's take Humanity Health Care, a fictional name that I'll give to a big not-for-profit charitable hospital chain here in Chicago. We are suing Humanity for overcharging the uninsured—for charging them twice what they charge you or me.

Ms. J, our client, had to pay $7,000 to give birth. If Blue Cross had insured her, Blue Cross would have paid $3,500. But that's the rule. It's only fair, if you're poor, that a charity would charge more.

We even alleged that perhaps the charity should give charity care—for free.

"Well, it's the best suit I ever brought," I told a friend the other night. "From the day we filed, we started getting relief." Humanity acted better—at least until they could toss out our class action. After a year of litigation, they had tripled their charity care, Humanity is even suing fewer people. Just before our case, it was filing about fifty to sixty lawsuits *a month* against the poor, the lame, and the uninsured. In the year before we filed our suit, Humanity brought a total of 1,098 lawsuits in the circuit courts.

Even that's an undercount. When I say 1,098 lawsuits, I'm leaving out the suits that the doctors brought. Yes, I know, we have no good count of *all* collection suits, or only what a judge has called "anecdata," but it seems that hospitals sue patients far more than patients sue hospitals.

Of course these suits against the uninsured are terrifying. When a charitable hospital sues the uninsured, it uses shock and awe. For any given service, such as delivery of a baby, it seeks the full "charge master" price—the list price that no one else pays. Insurance companies pay a lower negotiated rate. Blue Cross or Humana pay about a third.

Then, using this spurious list price, the hospital has the gall to say: "Look how much we lose when we have to treat these people!" That is, they press a phony price on the most vulnerable in our society, the people they get a tax exemption to serve.

Pay up! Then in the courts their collection lawyers sigh: "Okay, we'll give you a discount."

That's their charity: to cut down the price to something that is probably bigger than what the insurance companies would pay. Then, God help them, people sign these payment plans.

Of course, they don't have the money to meet even this "reduced" payment plan. Imagine that you're living in Chicago, making $21,000 and trying to pay for housing for yourself and your child. Then the charity garnishes your wages.

Do you see why we're bringing the suit?

When the medical malpractice lawyers sue hospitals, they don't push the defendants into bankruptcy. By contrast, when charities sue, they do, often wrecking lives in the process. As Elizabeth Warren of Harvard points out in *The Two-Income Trap*, the biggest single reason why Americans file for bankruptcy is that a hospital or a doctor is suing on a bill.

In 2005, our country had personal bankruptcy filings of 1.7 million! For many of these filings, we can thank our doctors and hospitals. I think the number would and should be much higher, but people go into hiding. Or they leave the country. Or they already filed for bankruptcy and can't file for eight more years.

It is hard to measure all the litigation that our charities generate directly and indirectly. The National Center for State Courts does not break out a count of "collection" cases as such for the seventeen states it tracks. But lately, in these states, it's reporting a big rise in state court "contract" cases. It's very likely these are assembly-line collection cases, mostly default judgments from people with medical and other bills.

In terms of sheer legal carnage, then, the hospitals are far worse than the trial lawyers. But Howard's book, *The Death of Common Sense*, has not a word about the hospitals and doctors suing "in contract."

Of course, these aren't contracts. In our case against Humanity, no one ever signed a contract at all. Humanity picks any price it likes, and then effectively negotiates the *real* contract in court, by threat and intimidation.

So when patients get the chance to sue hospitals, why should they act with restraint? It is too simple to say that in the area of medical malpractice, patients are just dishing it back. It is now part of the culture, I fear, the culture of Winner Take All. And the hospitals and doctors, with their feverish squeezing of patients, are as responsible as any for the legal culture we have.

How did this happen? In part, I could blame this on the collapse of unions. People lost the right to bargain. Employers cut back. Now more and more are uninsured or underinsured, with deductibles of $5,000. In the United States today, only six out of ten employers even offer health insurance, according to the Kaiser Foundation.

Meanwhile, the charities have stopped providing charity. The Great Society passed Medicare and Medicaid. By 1970, it seemed that the need for such "charity," or free care for the poor, would disappear.

Then we lost the unions. Today it's often the middle class that needs some kind of charity. But that old charity, the Mother Cabrini type, is gone. Today, she is more likely to be running Hewlett Packard.

Who's replaced her? It's an MBA getting $400,000 a year, and probably a second salary off the books. And the hospital boards are full of businessmen who are there not to help the poor but to get contracts for their corporations.

You and I know that MBAs aren't bad people. But they want their money. They're the ones baying for all the litigation against the uninsured.

Still, according to the *Newsweek* article "Lawsuit Hell," the enemy of the people is, over and over again, some poor guy filing a tort.

A kid whose leg was amputated, but it was the wrong leg.

A nurse who claims she was unlawfully fired: age, race, handicap, etc.

And *Newsweek* says, in effect: Blame the little people, not the hospitals, which are bringing far more suits. And then goes on to pay homage to Philip Howard. But then *Columbia Journalism Review* did a major exposé—it claimed that *Newsweek* was then paying a fee to Howard's firm to defend it in a civil rights suit brought by *Newsweek*'s own reporters.

Perhaps it's only the hospital that has made a shambles of the law of trusts.

I fear not.

In the United States today, the university may be even worse. That's the other great charitable institution dating back to the Middle Ages. No, I am not about to write in the manner of Foucault. I'd only note that, like the hospital, the university is turning into Frankenstein. It's hard to believe that the university was once a penniless thing, begging, with barely enough to even feed the monks. Now it seems to rival the Standard Oil Trust. Taken as a whole, Harvard and the other Great Universities are on a par with Wal-Mart. This type of charity preys not just on the students and their parents but on every one of us, even the very poor. Yes, a Harvard, MIT, or Stanford preys not just on the rich but even on working people. They are tax-exempt, so they diminish the tax base of the cities, where the poor line up for food from pantries. In the form of bequests and gifts, they get even more of the national wealth, tax-exempt, for which the working poor also end up paying. They also get billions in financial aid, billions upon billions, directly from the federal and state governments.

Like charitable hospitals, they can also issue bonds tax-exempt at lower rates of interest. They get privileged access to private capital.

What do these universities do in return? They proceed without legal restraint to gouge people at every income level and way of life. Obviously, they gouge their own students. In most of Europe students go to college for free. There is no tuition. In every developed country but the United States (and soon our one ally, the UK), the university operates in some capacity as a charity.

A student in Europe often has a civil right to go to college for free. Students here have no such right. And I'm not arguing here for such a right. But even under our system, we should have a right to require the university to act more charitably in dealing with the young.

Let's begin with tuition. Why should a tax-exempt not-for-profit institution be free, legally, to charge a tuition of $40,000 or $50,000 a year? I am waiting for someone to sue to impose a cap. Yes, the tax exemption is for an "educational" purpose; but back when these tax exemptions were put in place, education was a form of charity. Where is the charity here? Maybe the argument is this: those who benefit should have to pay their share. Then why give the exemption in the first place? For Bennington College and their ilk, we as taxpayers, in various ways, direct and indirect, already carry a tax burden that is at least equal to that of taxpayers in countries where the schools are free. We deserve a benefit: equal opportunity for young people of talent. This was one of the causes of the French Revolution—the lack of a charitable benefit to allow for a "career open to talent." It's disgraceful enough that even the nobility have to pay $40,000 a year or more: yes, it is unjust even for the nation's rich. But worse by far, the middle class have to pay this too—indeed, not only pay it, but have their children take out loans in order to do so.

Not small loans, either. Big ones.

In 1993, the average borrower had $9,272 in debt. Today the average borrower has $19,210 in debt. Of course, many are at public schools.

And the kids who go to private lenders are often not the ones going to Bennington. They can't even dream of going to the elite schools. But it's galling for the rest of us to subsidize, with our tax money, this whole structure of inequality.

Which are worse—private or public universities? It makes no difference. We subsidize them both. And yes, the public universities are catching up.

It is not just that the private elite schools are cheating these kids; they are cheating the rest of us who pay the taxes too. Like every other American, I am taxed as truly to pump up a Brown or a Stanford as I am taxed in my own state for various public schools. And I am taxed for the loans to the kids so they can pay out these unconscionable tuitions. I would be glad to subsidize even the private schools if the kids who graduate gave back something to society. But if the kids leave the elite schools with too much debt—and I am thinking here of the middle-class kids—it's likely they won't, or can't, pay back anything to society: they have to pay off their loans. So they veer away from real charity, or teaching, or public service. They go out and prey upon others, just as the "charitable" university has preyed upon them. It's because the kids have to pay it back that we have so little sense of public service in our culture.

It's true for lawyers. Kids often come out of law school with over $80,000 in debt. As my friend Dan Morrissey, a former law school dean, points out, except for the top 10 or 15 percent, lawyers don't make much money. In a kind of hell themselves, the kids have every incentive to spread the hell to others.

Indeed, I blame the tuitions charged by our law schools for

making the legal profession so nasty. Those who really shape the values of these kids are not the professors like Mr. Chips but the hustlers chasing down the student loans. Alas, late in life, I learned a lot about these collection agencies. In Chicago or St. Louis or Seattle, you'll find three or four big ones. They fight each other viciously to see who can squeeze the most from kids. How do I know? We sued one. It was a sexual harassment case. No surprise: these places are set up to harass. Some of the collectors become superstars. They make $500,000 or more in commissions. They're approachable guys, in the sense that they're always in the singles bars.

They are the true bounty hunters of the age. And the bounties are big. The hustlers get collection fees of up to 25 percent. We the taxpayers end up subsidizing these guys, who roam the singles bars at night. And of course, they phone, they sue, they garnish wages.

In other words, they're like hospitals.

With one big difference: Hospitals only sue the poor and the sick. Student loan collectors go after kids with MBAs and law degrees, and that should worry us, because one day the prey will become the predators. It's all summed up in a piece I once read by a man named Roger Roots. By any market standard, he says, it's not a loan that makes any real sense. "A student loan is, in effect, a 'mortgage on the debtor's future,' rather than a true commercial transaction."

It's also a mortgage on our country, and the whole nation loses out. When kids have to scramble to make as much as they can, we all have to pay it back. After paying off these indentures, who is going to feel an obligation to give back to society? To the extent that universities abandon their charitable mission and prey upon their students, we end up with more people who prey upon us all. We end up with a meaner society.

·   ·   ·

But there are more direct ways that universities now prey upon the country.

Here's one. A university can now patent a "breakthrough" drug that we the taxpayers paid for it to develop. Then it can sell the drug back to the taxpayers at monopoly prices.

Consider this charitable-mission outrage. A university receives a tax exemption, in part so it can do scientific and medical research to benefit the public. In addition, we taxpayers pay the university, directly, with grants, to do such research. But now under the Bayh-Dole Act, the university can patent its research—the research we gave them a tax exemption, and then a grant, to do. It's research that we funded, *twice*. In return, the university goes out and reaps a huge profit on its monopoly.

Ever wonder why these universities have so much money? This is a big part of it.

By what legal or constitutional authority do these schools and professors get a patented monopoly right for research that they get paid double by the public to carry out in the first place? There's no authority in the Constitution. As set out in Article I, Section 8, the purpose of the patent clause is a narrow one; it is to encourage "Inventors" to bring their discoveries into the public domain. Yet taxpayer-funded research is already in the public domain. It makes no sense to let a university take out a patent to charge a price for this drug that no taxpayer can pay. But that's what happens. Either that or they license it to the big drug companies.

Then the university *and* the drug company rip everyone off—again, for a taxpayer-funded discovery.

Fearing lawsuits, a few drug companies have brought down the superinflated prices that they charge only to the uninsured. But even at the "normal" prices, the drug barons and universities can go on soaking those of us who have insurance. Harvard. The University of Illinois. The University of Chicago. Under the guise of being charities, they plunder America.

With the power to charge a monopoly price, the university essentially has the power to "tax" the public. It is much like the old system of tax monopolies in Bourbon France. Think of the tax on salt. In a similar way, a university imposes a tax on drugs. That is, it can charge a monopoly price.

But at least in Bourbon France, those who engaged in these kinds of tax monopolies were not set up as charities. That's the outrage—these are our charities. Of all the various bodies of law, it's the law of trusts, today, that is most in shambles, or so it seems to me. But perhaps administrative law is worse.

CHAPTER 4

From Administrative Law
to No Law

The Rise of the Whistle-Blower
and the Trial Lawyer

I slipped into law school at the very end of the post–New Deal era, but already kids were dropping out of administrative law. They were taking trial practice instead. We had already begun deregulating.

Now, instead of administrative law, or public law, we have tort law, or private law. We have our private bar—the hated trial lawyers—to do what civil servants used to do. By that I mean that the government became weaker after 1972. We began wave after wave of deregulation—not just economic deregulation, but deregulation of public safety: worker safety, food safety, transportation safety.

There's no reason to learn about the Administrative Procedure Act because administrative agencies don't do much anymore. Now, some may object: "Wait, I don't think we deregulated everything! Maybe energy, and maybe telecoms. But what do you mean, we deregulated safety?"

I know, more liberal hysteria. Okay, I *am* hysterical about it.

Deregulation doesn't always happen formally. It can happen just by defunding regulation. As the great law professor Clyde Summers used to try to teach kids like me, "It costs a lot of money for people to have 'rights.' "

Over and over we have gutted the funding of regulation. Think of the deficits since Reagan—and now Bush! The deficits plot the degree of our deviation from the Rule of Law. What the numbers tell us is not of any shortfall in entitlements, because legally none can occur; rather, deficits trigger a shortfall in the execution of the laws. Deficits turn into cuts in discretionary spending, especially for lawyers, regulators, and administrative judges—not to mention the inspectors of worker safety, food safety, automobile safety, drug safety, rail safety, flood control, even homeland security. Because we regard the Rule of Law as if it were a free lunch, as if it costs nothing to execute the law, we fail to grasp what the numbers are telling us. In a single year it's hard to see. But every year, Congress cuts a little more out of the discretionary budget. Less money. Fewer people. And now to make sure the civil servants don't even ask for money, Congress has started to prohibit unions. They started this process in the Department of Homeland Security. All of this underfunding has the effect of scaring talented people away from public service. And with whopping student loans, the ones who used to go into public service are staying out anyway. We have lost a whole generation of talented people in this way, and now the government itself seems more inept.

Let me give a small example. During the last Bush-Kerry debate, the CBS man asked, "What about the shortage of the vaccine for the flu?" Of course, Bush could only mumble. Kerry ducked it too. He talked instead about his plan for health insurance. But I wish Kerry had said, "Yeah, the government screwed it up. What do you expect? We don't get good people in the government anymore. Or the ones we have are overworked. Look, if we don't want to pay to have a decent civil service—and by the way, decent law enforcement—this is what we're going to get."

And as we keep gutting the public sector, we'll see panics like this more and more.

Over and over in my practice I see the evils of deregulation, both the open and the covert kind. And since I don't really do administrative law, if *I* can see these evils, they must be epidemic. Let me pick a few.

Work

The Labor Department, which I know best, seems to me the saddest case. I could pick any office—OSHA, ERISA, any one. But let's take minimum wage. All over the country, people at Wal-Mart have been working off the clock, for free. And who knows what's happening in the back, in the smaller places!

There's no one in the field to investigate.

It's not the government but private lawyers who have been bringing suits. Yet we lawyers can't even find the worst cases. I mean the people who are in slavery, including "white" slavery, or forced prostitution. And why can't we find them? Same answer: there's no one in the field.

Once, when I filed a suit to get the Labor Department to enforce the child labor laws for sixteen- and seventeen-year-olds, kids they don't even pretend to protect, I got nowhere. I met with the solicitor, who told me: "Look, suppose I say I agree with you. How would I ever get the money to enforce it?"

He was right. If I had won and they had issued regulations, it would only have been worse. In Labor, and in agency after agency, we have a vast complex body of regulatory law—

which could take a mandarin ten years to learn—that no one enforces. The law is there—on paper. A lot of paper. How much? Fifty volumes, in paperback—I counted. But for big chunks of these volumes, there's no one to enforce it.

What is the equivalent of fifty volumes in paper airplanes?

So it's left to the private sector, to ordinary citizens, to figure out some way to take the law into their hands. Instead of civil servants, we look to vigilantes. In particular, we look to trial lawyers, who are in it for the money and cherry-pick the good cases. Or in the case of many Labor Department regulations, we look to our working poor, to maids and parking valets, who, we hope, will one day decide to blow the whistle—do something, scream—even if they're fired. What's replaced the civil servant? The whistleblower. Instead of the Rule of Law, we now have these tiny acts of martyrdom and rage.

Health

Or let's take patient safety. As I represent nurses, I can see, in this one area, how the Rule of Law is in shambles. Why?

Hospitals are cutting back on nurses. That's how the MBAs are driving up profit. The nurse-to-patient ratio is ballooning. Patients sit in ERs for hours. It takes longer to start the orders. Sure, Medicare has lots of regulations telling hospitals what to do—but there are not enough nurses to carry them out. Or civil servants to enforce them. Who knows? There may not be enough trial lawyers to bring the medical malpractice cases! At any rate it galls me to hear the president rail about trial lawyers suing hospitals. Why is it that the trial lawyers bring these suits? Because the hospitals depart from a standard of care, often set out in federal regulations, that the president of the United States has the duty to enforce. And why do the hospitals depart from a standard of care?

Not enough nurses on the floor. And not enough inspectors.

Indeed, we are handing over enforcement to private organizations like the Joint Commission on Accreditation of Hospitals, which are answerable to the hospitals themselves.

If the president wanted to cripple the lawyers, he might consider, for example, setting nurse-to-patient ratios and actually enforcing them. Of course, he won't. Yet as hospitals cut back on nurses, they end up violating more standards and regulations.

Result? More and more patients die. A study in the *Journal of the American Medical Association* counted up the dead: in the hospitals that have eight patients for each nurse instead of four in their medical-surgical units, the chance of any one patient dying goes up 31 percent. And that's just where the hospitals are cutting back.

In fact they tell spouses: Why don't you sleep over?

Bring on the trial lawyers! Because when the Rule of Law really is in shambles, that's what people get. When we have no contract, we get tort. And when we have no trust law, we get tort. And when we deregulate, we get tort, as well. One can calculate the rise of tort from the drop in the numbers of those who simply watch over us, from the civil servant inspector to the nurse on the floor.

With the decline in administrative law, I have become a kind of tort lawyer, too. I run with the vigilantes—or at least I file a suit or two for them. I think of P, a nurse who works at Q. At least, she did until the hospital fired her. She was a red hot pepper of a whistle blower. She fired up the nurses. She urged them to file "assignment-despite-objection forms" by the dozens. I-am-working-under-protest-because-there-aren't-enough-nurses-to-cover-patients. And all over the state, yes, the state of Illinois, she set up hearings for a patient safety act. And she sent off petitions to get state officials to come look at conditions at the Q Hospital.

Which, at last, they did.

In other words she is working for us, the public, like a private attorney general. She is doing it without pay, and soon without her job!

When the hospital fired her, I filed suit. Oh, the hospital hates her, calls her a liar, and threatens to sue her for libel. Sure, a battle like this is even fun sometimes, I must admit. Like at her deposition. It went on all day. I had a little fun, seeing the way the hospital lawyer dished it out to her—and then seeing the way she dished it back. Both were very good. Yes, at moments, I enjoy an eight-hour deposition.

Otherwise, it was just another day in hell.

In any event, is this what now passes for the Rule of Law in the United States—a nurse has to pour gasoline over herself and strike a match to get the attention of a public health official? And then she has to fight for her reputation because the hospital makes *her* the issue?

But that's just patient safety. There's another area even worse.

Public Safety

Like meat inspection. How could regulation be collapsing here? I am now in a legal battle where we have to prove that the Department of Agriculture bothers to enforce the law at all.

Does that sound surreal? It sure does. But let me tell you about our suit with the owner of a chicken-processing plant. We are suing for his workers, under the so-called WARN Act, which requires a notice before a plant closing. In this case, the owner did not give the required sixty days' notice before he closed the plant. "But the Department of Agriculture shut me down," the owner argues. "How could I foresee that?" He argues that yes, he may have done bad things, and let rats run wild, and let rats shit on the chicken meat. And yes, it is even true that the inspectors of the Department of Agriculture gave him write-ups.

But here is the issue: Was it reasonable for the owner to foresee that the Department of Agriculture would enforce its own regulations?

He had an argument: "I'm in the business, and they never enforce the law." Never. That was his claim. The Department of Agriculture is more or less a joke. Under Bush I, then Clinton, and then Bush II, it's gotten worse. "Everyone knows!" Now comes the ruling of the district judge, who is a liberal, a Clinton appointee: Yes, he says, it was unforeseeable. It was as if he took judicial notice that as a matter of common knowledge, the government does not enforce the laws.

Case dismissed!

I'm still in shock that the employer got away with such an argument. But he had a point. We cut back on inspectors. We don't impose fines. So he had no way of knowing that the Department of Agriculture would shut him down.

In other words, the application of the Rule of Law is the equivalent of an act of God. Completely arbitrary. Like a hurricane.

Yes, we appealed. I helped edit the brief. It was not my case, but my colleague's. All I did was strike out the word "rodent" and put in the word "rat." And the word "rat" came up a lot because the plant was filthy: full of rats and rat droppings all over the meat. The scary part was that the plant had gone on like this for years. The more we deregulate, and the more the inspectors are told not to threaten but to work in a "cooperative spirit," the more the rodents, and the rats, are free to go on dropping on our chicken wings and nuggets.

So what happened on appeal? Well, of course we argued that

a judge cannot assume that it is "unforeseeable" for the laws ever to be enforced. In the United States, has the Rule of Law really come to this? Even though we got the District Court judgment reversed, we did not really win the point.

Instead, we have to go to trial. We have to have a trial to determine whether the owner of the chicken-processing plant has to believe the government when it says to him they're going to enforce the law.

Again, it's not just patient safety or food safety—it's *any* kind of safety. Lately I have been representing locomotive engineers, and it's even true of rail safety. Rail safety! People are dying at rail crossings. But now we curb the inspectors! On November 7 and 14, 2004, the *New York Times* ran two front-page stories about how the Federal Railroad Administration is going easy on Union Pacific. The acting FRA administrator—who resigned after the *Times* broke the stories on safety violations—said that the agency had a "partnership" with Union Pacific. Instead of enforcing the law, we let our "partner" decide.

And here, too, we have whistle-blowers. I mean literally— our clients, the engineers! But they can only blow the whistle if they can hold on to their licenses. The FRA has now let Union Pacific snatch their licenses, without a hearing or any due process at all.

What about the federal regulations that require hearings? Well, naturally, we sued. These regulations are on the books. Here's FRA's defense: it has no "lawfully constituted" power to enforce these regulations. Never mind that these regulations have been on the books for decades. As of July 2006, the FRA decided, with no warning, not to enforce them anymore.

Meanwhile, the accidents go up, but we must not upset our "partner," Union Pacific.

Rail safety, for God's sake! How nice if it were just the New Deal that was in shambles. But in the United States today, even the Square Deal is in shambles. I mean, the regulatory state as it existed under Theodore—not Franklin—Roosevelt. Sure, I'd like to curb the tort lawyers—because I hate to see the law turn into tort. But without the tort lawyers, I might be dead. A train wreck. A spill of deadly gas.

The last line of defense is the type of people who sue tobacco companies.

In Chicago, I'm living in a ring of nuclear power plants. I'd be in terrible danger if we tried to curb the tort lawyers. It's only the tort system that saves us from a Three Mile Island. Yes, it might be nice if we had more nuclear plants. We could cut down on Mid East oil. And if I lived in France, with all its nuclear energy, I might think it a good thing. So why do I oppose it here? Because France has a real administrative state, a real civil service, and the best and brightest do the regulating. In the United States, we can't even keep the trains on the tracks.

As a citizen, I'd like to curb our trial lawyers. But I also want to live.

You may well scoff at the specter of a Three Mile Island, a Bhopal, or even, God forbid, a Chernobyl. Perhaps none of that would happen even if we curbed the trial lawyers. But consider what happened in one case where we did put the lid on trial lawyers.

Corporate Finance

Enron. World Com. How did it happen? We got rid of administrative law and then tort law. Then the whole thing blew up. Here is how I tried to explain it a few months ago, at lunch, to my lawyer friend Mary.

"First, in stage one, we had the SEC, the Securities and Exchange Commission. The New Deal. Joe Kennedy. We got the best, the brightest. We regulated like hell.

"Then, in stage two, we got deregulation. We cut back enforcement. Instead of the New Deal, we got the New Deal Lite.

"Then comes stage three, the tort lawyers. With Reagan, they move in. They start to file a lot of class actions, for nondisclosure and fraud. Corporate people say, 'Stop!'

"So fine, in stage four we stop it. We get the Contract with America. Newt Gingrich, the Congress, they pass a few laws, to cut back the lawyers suing over stock fraud. Corporate people are happy.

"So then, stage five: Ka boom! Enron. World Com. It's Three Mile Island. Everything blows up.

"So now, in stage six, we have Sarbanes-Oxley. We make CEOs sign balance sheets with statements like, 'I do not engage in fraud.' But is that enough? No. So what else did we do?

"We turned it over to Eliot Spitzer, the Attorney General of New York. A state Attorney General, even if the state is New York! He sues the banks and the big companies. I mean, the leading regulator of not just the United States but the *whole world economy* suddenly became the state Attorney General in New York. I like Eliot Spitzer. Thank God for him.

"But the Attorney General of one state? Every three or four years we have a new legal paradigm. We get the SEC, then tort, then laissez-faire, then self-regulation, and then a state Attorney General. It's all in shambles."

Mary paused, and then she said: "It's like a boiler, isn't it? You try to cap the pressure in one place, and it blows up somewhere else."

Yes, she said it: We get rid of the New Deal, the old administrative law, and now we are about to get rid of tort. Guess what's going to happen? The boiler's going to blow.

Mary's right. What happened at Enron or World Com is just as likely to happen in the ER or at a Mr. Chicken outlet or on a rotting railroad track. I hate the way the old administrative law is in a meltdown into tort, but I'd rather have a tort than nothing at all.

If the breakdowns in patient safety or food safety or rail safety do not convince you that the regulatory state is now in shambles, and if the legal anarchy in corporate finance is not enough to do it either, then I ask you to consider one final case.

Payday Loans

With the payday loan stores, we have gone from administrative law to no law. We've hit bottom: no Rule of Law at all.

I got involved in a suit against payday loan "stores"; otherwise, I doubt I would even have noticed them. Because of my hero, the late Monsignor Jack Egan, I went on a committee to go after payday loans. I ended up filing a suit, which turned out to be mainly a cri de coeur. (I mean, we lost.) But first let me explain what a payday loan is, and why it is such an emblem of the collapse of regulation.

Let's say I'm making $30,000 a year, I have a family, and I'm short $200 this month. I go to you, Mr. Payday Loan. Now, I don't literally turn over my next paycheck. But in return for $200, I write you a postdated check for $240.

I know, you know, and the state of Illinois knows that at the moment I write this check, it's a bad check. It may be postdated, but under the revised Uniform Commercial Code, my bank is allowed to cash it now, right away, as soon as I write it.

Right away, I have set myself up. You can prosecute. If they cash my check, I won't have the money to cover it. So to avoid the prosecution, I have to take out another and even bigger loan.

And another.

And another.

I keep writing bad checks, and I keep giving you more and more power to put me into jail. Soon I can owe $1,000 for a loan of just $200. Even the mob with a juice loan hesitates, I believe, to overreach like that.

I have to admit, at the beginning I was annoyed with Father Egan for dragging me into these meetings and paying so much attention to this one little issue of payday loans. Come on! This was a priest who had marched for civil rights. He was a kind of 1960s hero. Isn't there bigger stuff to take on than these stupid payday loans? But it slowly dawned on me what is so awful about the damned things, emblematically.

What is awful and so different from a mob loan is that the state of Illinois is working as a kind of silent partner. The state of Illinois has to license every lender that charges more than the official state ceiling on interest—a ceiling of 9 percent. Yes, in the old days before deregulation, there were usury laws. On paper, there still is a cap—incredibly, of 9 percent. But the cap applies to no one. The state gives a license to virtually anyone who wants to exceed the cap. Now, the old law, still on the books, says that the state has to investigate the "reputation" of each applicant for "honesty" and "fairness," and shall not issue a license unless it finds the reputation assures the state the applicant will be honest and fair. That's literally the law. But the state has never conducted any such investigation. As "honest" and "fair" lenders, it gives licenses to people who charge up to 2,000 percent!

So the state is in effect a business partner with every payday lender. It says in effect: "We the state of Illinois find it honest and fair to charge 2,000 percent." It's true that a group of us reformers tried to pass a law to limit payday lending. It led to nothing. There was a new law to limit payday lenders who made loans of less than 120 days to charge no more than 400 percent. Does 400 percent sound like a victory? Even so, the payday lenders just laughed. They immediately began to make loans for 121 days and charge whatever interest they pleased.

Because some of the big banks own the payday lenders, no one in the state has done anything to stop this. They keep issuing the licenses for lenders to make loans of 2,000 percent. It is true that in eleven states, there is some limit like 400 percent on these loans. But most states do nothing. They are too weeak. If they pass a law there is a huge loophole. So these mob loans, juice loans, authorized by the state, go on and on from sea to shining sea. Our government is a silent partner in this scamming.

In our time, government is actually licensing extortion. People sign postdated checks. While there are few actual prosecutions, the consumers who sign the checks don't know that. They not only agree to roll over the loans at rates of 400 to 2,000 percent interest, but they do it in terror. Maybe a state will prosecute if the check bounces. It probably won't—but who knows? Soon enough, you can owe $2,000 on a $200 loan.

"But people need the money." Yes, there are no safety nets provided by government anymore, except the payday loans. Why don't the states let the big banks sell heroin as well through these payday loan stores? The poor could use the heroin as solace for their woes. All right, it's a serious objection. If the states did pull the licenses of banks that overreached or did not act honestly and fairly as required by the older law, there might be a limit to the abuses. That seems hopeless, of course. The state is too weak to stand up to the banks.

CHAPTER 5

The Deregulation of Public Space

Or, the End of Equity

One reason the Rule of Law has collapsed is the retreat from injunctive relief, or what in law school we used to call the "structural injunction." By that I mean the way federal courts used to order broad changes for hospitals, prisons, parks.

Then we cut back this "judicial activism." And as is usually the case whenever legal conservatives succeed in curbing the courts, this led to a huge explosion in litigation. The result? We went from equity to tort. We went from one big case for an injunction to a thousand little cases for individual damages.

Consider lawsuits against the cops. That's one of the big examples in the *Newsweek* special, "Litigation Hell." Too many lawyers are soaking the cities. For what? Police brutality, of course. My own mayor, Richard Daley, is quoted in *Newsweek*, with his usual eloquence, on the drain of public funds. It seems it costs the city money when the police engage in beatings, the random killing of innocent motorists, and the occasional act of systematic human torture. If torture in Chicago sounds far-fetched, you can just read the write-ups by our local reporters.

Now, prior to his statement in *Newsweek*, I had thought Mayor Daley was in favor of all these suits. A radio reporter had asked him: "Why does Chicago have so many more complaints than New York about police brutality?" And here is Daley's answer, more or less: It's because things are so much better in Chicago. Out here, people aren't afraid to complain the way they are in New York. And if we have more complaints, it only shows our city is better run. People in Chicago have more confidence in the local government.

That's why we lead the country in complaints about police brutality. It's our way of expressing our trust in Mayor Daley.

But in *Newsweek*, he took a different view. He griped about the suits, and how the tort lawyers got too much in damages. Yes, he's right. It does cost too much. I'm a taxpayer, and it galls me to pay even my small share of it.

On the other hand, we "lawyers on the left" tried to enjoin the worst police practices in cases like *Los Angeles v. Lyons*. Instead of damages in tort, we tried to get court orders to stop the way they treated prisoners. But in *Lyons*, the U.S. Supreme Court, urged on by cities like Chicago, ended the chance for doing that. The Court held that Mr. Lyons had no standing to file for an injunction once he had been beaten up and let go. He had no stake in a "live controversy," as we lawyers say, at least with respect to future beatings by the cops. How likely was it that Mr. Lyons would be beaten up again? Only a legal conservative could talk like this: "Oh, he has no interest now." It's argued that one-time victims don't care anymore about what happens in the future. ("Hey, I've already been beaten senseless. This new case has nothing to do with me!") So no one can sue to stop the problem. And if no one can sue, there is no way a judge has the power to fix it. See? Los Angeles won! As a result, the beatings can go on and on. No injunctions!

As a result, the lawsuits for damages go on and on. And the drain on city treasuries go on and on. We can thank the legal conservatives. We can thank Reagan, and Bush I, and Bush II. Because of them, we stopped the "legal activism" that could have ended all this nonsense by an injunction in a single case.

But that's only one little effect—more beatings by cops. We also ended up with more disorder in the streets. We already had enough, just from the rise of poverty in our cities. Yet at this very moment, we are cutting back on the judicial remedies—injunctions—that help to keep some order in our public spaces. In the 1960s, under civil rights laws, federal judges had begun to order cities not only to open up public facilities to minorities but to spend money on them.

More money meant they fixed up pools and parks.

More money meant they sent in more city workers.

And more city workers meant more "eyes on the streets," to use the phrase of Jane Jacobs in *The Death and Life of Great American Cities*. Yes: more money. To fix the broken windows. To make the places nicer. By the mid-1970s, just as the golden age of inner-city poverty had started, the courts were issuing injunctions to guard the public space, which meant spending more on the schools, the parks, city services. As Rudy Giuliani would later discover, it would have been a good thing if we had fixed the broken windows. But at the worst possible moment, all of this stopped.

We began curbing the injunctions. The liberal judges left. The right wing came to power. We could have used civil law to keep the cities safer. Instead, by scrapping the injunctions, we just got more disorder.

Instead of regulating public space, we deregulated it. As we retreated from this use of equity, we turned to the criminal law instead. From 1980 on it seems like that's all we've been doing.

It's as if we're trying to put everyone in prison. Paradoxically, by locking up so many, we may have made the public spaces even more dangerous.

How?

There were fewer adult males on the street. By age thirty-five or forty, they might have been a force for order, or restraint. But they disappeared not for five or ten years but for twenty to forty years. Worse, prison is often a way of creating crime—for gang life, prison is a kind of oxygen. It keeps more men in gangs longer; it extends, not ends, membership in a gang. But now the gangs have to reach out and use children as couriers. The more men we sent into prison, the lower the age that kids began to kill. That can't be a coincidence. Thanks to the gangs, which directed things from the prisons, fourteen- to eighteen-year-olds now became their couriers. Kids ran the drugs. Soon, thanks to the mindless lockup, kids took the lead in killing. Here was the real blowback in the "war on crime." Kids, being kids, were even wilder in their violence; one might say that children are more childish in the way they kill. They shot the wrong kids. They shot at little girls on porches. They shot at traffic lights. They shot in school yards. They shot in places where adults, even young adults in their twenties, even sick and psychopathic killers, would not have shot.

A city of armed children, shooting, had an effect on higher-income types like me. After all, by 1993, in my own city the murder rate had reached ninety or more a month. Many of the ninety were kids, of course. Even if it was all in another part of town, even if it was mostly sixteen- or seventeen-year-olds who would never come after me, it changes the way we look at public space, not just in the inner city or the places where the poor are.

We all adjust in some way, big or small.

My barber told me the other day, "I dropped out of high school back then because I was afraid of being killed." If it had not been for murder, he might have had a much different life. Even some of my lawyer friends began to notice how many people were being killed, albeit in other neighborhoods. "Oh, it doesn't affect me," we might say, but when I go to Europe and see a young woman walking alone down a street late at night, I know it does. I'm startled. Here, even in nice neighborhoods, people don't feel safe out in the open. Even far, far out in the suburbs we keep our kids entombed in malls.

As this sense of disorder and randomness has increased, our standard of living has dropped—not so much in terms of private income, but in our access to public goods. Yes, the public parks are still there. And the public pools. There are even public concerts. And if we decide to use these things, we know we won't be shot.

Yet, somehow the public space is still not available. Sometimes, it's not geographically available, because we have to disperse or put huge distances between each other, out of fear of each other, even fear of being murdered. A concert I could attend if I lived in Hamburg is out of my reach if I live in St. Louis because we are always making detours or driving around places we might be murdered. Because the Rule of Law has collapsed in the inner city, public space and public goods are just not as available to me in the same way as before.

Who do I blame for the loss of these public goods? I blame some of it on the judicial conservatives, on judges who made it impossible to protect the public spaces. For starters, they blocked the use of structural injunctions. The Right screamed when activist judges tried to force cities to spend money—to fix the broken windows and clean up the garbage. (Later, police and crime experts realized this was just what we should have done.) But worse, our judicial conservatives blocked various attempts to stop the spread of handguns, especially to children. In the 1970s, when tort lawyers began to sue companies like Colt for negligence, the right-wing state judges carved out "exceptions" for the sale of handguns. Really, it was a kind of judicial activism by the right. For handguns, and only for handguns, they came up with rules that existed for no other consumer product. There is a duty of care in the sale or distribution of any product. But the judges decided that this Rule of Law did not apply to handguns. When it came to selling guns, it was impossible to be "negligent." Multiple sales to gangs (through straw purchasers). Mass sales at "gun fairs." The gun industry could do anything to put guns in the hands of criminals, or children.

Principles of negligence that would apply to a company like Coca-Cola did not apply to Colt. And this was not statutory or legislative but a judicially crafted exception, an exception to the ordinary principles of commercial law.

Even without bringing back the liberal Warren Court of the 1960s, we could have used the law to make it a bit safer to use the public space. Or so a few of us lawyers thought in the 1990s. Here's my own little story of what we tried to do.

When the murder rate hit ninety-five a month, and kids were shooting other kids on the playground, I decided I'd join a group of lawyers fighting handguns. We cooked up a tort suit to sue the gun industry for creating a classic public nuisance— for interfering with the use of public space. Since the courts had decided to gut the law of negligence in the sale of a handgun, this was the only good idea that we had left to us. It seemed to cry out, medievally, "Give me a try." The law of nuisance was an elderly type of common law, but maybe it could help the kids who were dying in the streets.

A public nuisance claim is one based on an ancient legal right, the right to use the public way without "interference," without unreasonable "apprehension"—without having to wonder, *Should I hit the dirt?* It is the right that you or I have to be unimpeded in any way, even by the way that some idiot in a red state wants to market guns. It is the right to be free of such things as a pigsty or a house full of prostitutes calling out to us, "Come over here and see us!" It is certainly the right to be free of smoke and noise. So why not the smoke and noise of guns, especially when they are being fired at us by kids?

We decided to sue. For Steve Young, whose son had been shot by another kid.

And then for Tony Ceriale, whose son, a young cop, had also died.

And then the city filed a suit as well. Yes, for all my criticism of Mayor Daley, he is my hero when it comes to handguns. And once the mayor had sued, other cities did as well. Not just the big ones, like New York, but even little ones, like Bridgeport, Connecticut.

Here was a chance to use the civil law to protect the public space before it was gone. Maybe, in a small way, this could create some civic trust all over America. And do away public rage.

But we lost. The funny thing is, we won at the trial level and the appellate level. Or at least we won the right to sue, to proceed to the taking of discovery, to the depositions. To poke around their house. On this right to proceed, we kept winning, until at last we hit the highest court in Illinois.

In November 2004, the Illinois Supreme Court issued a decision. We lost! The Illinois Supreme Court shut us down, seven to zero. They're elected, of course, and the ones from downstate are understandably afraid of the gun lobbies and the National Rifle Association. But we even lost the judges we elect from Chicago! We lost them all.

We lost. God, I hate being a lawyer.

All that rainy day, at the news boxes in the Loop, I had to see this headline over and over: BIG WIN FOR HANDGUN MANU-FACTURERS. What a month. Big win. Bush is reelected and the gun nuts win too.

Don't ever become a lawyer. Six years of my life—gone. Actually, for the last three or four I had little to do with the case. Others did the work, and I regard them as heroes, the best lawyers I know.

Don't ask me to give you a fair reading of the court's opinion—I couldn't do it. But let me note that there was a special concurrence from three of the justices, and let me put the gist of it into my own words, in a grossly unfair rendering:

"First, we are sorry about the murders. We really are. It really is terrible. And by the way, not only are we sorry about the murders—the allegations in your complaint are really scary. Wow! Did the gun companies really do this that you allege? My God, it probably does violate some kind of law. But you guys can't just come into court like this! We've got a modern regulatory state, you know? Please, you're putting us in a spot. Go to the legislature! They're elected. Of course, we're elected too, but . . ."

So that's what it boiled down to, in effect: "We're just the Illinois Supreme Court. We're just from Illinois. Go away! Go away! All you want to do is scare us!"

Oh, I know many will say, "Well, they're right, aren't they? You *should* go to the legislature." And I know the other objections: "There are already so many guns out there. What does this suit do about that?" And finally: "Do you really think Congress would let this suit go forward?" Even in the last session,

Congress nearly passed a bill to block these handgun suits. It may still have to pass it, because the public nuisance claim won in Ohio.

Yes, my home town of Cincinnati won in the Ohio Supreme Court—but then disgracefully dropped the case.

I know, I know. Maybe it *was* futile. But let me tell you why I think we should have brought it anyway: to make the judges do what the judges in the Weimar Republic failed to do, to say that murder in the streets is murder. We at least ought to be able to use the courts to make a record of what is going on. The Illinois Supreme Court refuses to let us even make a record of the murders. "Well, forget this old common law," some would say. "We have the modern administrative state."

But that modern administrative state is also the court. And we weren't really invoking the ancient law. We were invoking the way we used injunctions in the 1960s.

We lost. Meanwhile, thanks to their Big Win, the handgun manufacturers will go on selling and the mindless lockups will continue, no matter what the rate of crime. Our "modern" administrative state keeps growing: more prosecutors, more prison officials, more prison guards. Not to mention the other prison-related workers, like the laundry workers or the food service workers, some of them laid off by the airlines—they need jobs as well. These days there is a whole bureaucracy that needs a constant supply of new indictments and prosecutions. Even if the crime rate drops, we have to keep on prosecuting about the same number of people.

At least, it's true in Cook County.

I sometimes take friends to see Cook County jail, which is the biggest factory on the South Side now that we've shut the mills. When I first came out to Chicago in 1976, the jail had only two divisions. Now it's up to twelve. Mostly, it houses people waiting trial. Although the crime rate dropped to a new low, in 2003 the number of indictments hit a new high. We have to feed the monster. The prosecutors, the cops, the food service workers—we all need our jobs.

Besides, it may well be that the lockup did bring down the crime rate. At least, no one can disprove it. It may always be unclear why the rate dropped all at once in so many different types of cities, from New York to Topeka, all across the land. At some point in the 1990s, it seemed to happen all at once. If the economist Richard Freeman is right as to what pushed the rate of crime up, it's probably fair to say what brought it down: the minimum wage finally went up. At least, the timing of it works. Congress raised it about a year before the drop in crime began. Raising it to $5.15 pushed up other hourly wages too, since many wages track the minimum and many companies pay the minimum wage "plus."

Indeed, the lockup may have helped push up wages too. When the job market tightened even a little, the wages of the poor shot up—because so many potential workers were in jail or prison. That's why welfare reform "worked," or seemed to at first. Otherwise the moms would never have found jobs. Fortunately their husbands and their boyfriends were in prison.

If it pushed up wages, the lockup probably did bring the rate of crime down. Even in Chicago, people are starting to come outside again. We have a big new park on the lake. Parents with their children are showing up at outdoor concerts. It's nice. Except, in real terms, the wages of the poor have been dropping again, slowly.

And if that's true, children, let's put the chicken back in the picnic basket. That's the stake in rushing to get the minimum wage back up.

CHAPTER 6

The War on Reason, Uniformity, and Predictability in the Law
Why the Right Hates Class Action

Next to trial lawyers, Bush and the GOP seem most to hate class actions. Indeed, they seem to hate trial lawyers because they do file class actions. In the 2004 campaign, Bush and Cheney spoke a bizarre amount about class actions—especially the ones filed in Madison County, in my own state, Illinois. Yes, the New Right hates class actions. It's not even that they hate "little," or state, class actions; rather, they hate the big ones, the national class actions. It's odd, on its face. Why shouldn't a class action against a global business like Wal-Mart be nationwide? It would seem to make perfect sense.

"That is not a role for the states," said the president.

So the president campaigned against "national" class actions filed in "state" courts to regulate "global" businesses, such as Wal-Mart and the like. "How terrible that the states allow this." But at least in the area of consumer fraud, the state courts allow these suits only because the federal government itself does not. There is no federal law against consumer fraud. There is no federal class action that anyone can bring—

especially now that the courts have virtually nullified federal antitrust law, which used to be a kind of law against consumer fraud. These class actions arose only because federal regulation broke down, especially in stopping business from ripping off their customers.

A few months after the 2004 election, a Republican Congress did pass the Class Action Fairness Act (CAFA). (After CAFA came Bush's debacle over Social Security privatization, and then Katrina, and the worsening war, and his administration began melting down. Strange that CAFA may be the only big law in his second term, other than stripping detainees of habeas corpus and other rights.)

The nominal purpose of CAFA is to stop the ambush of global giants in sleepy hollow state courts. But the upshot will be to deregulate fraud. Or at least it will be much harder to resolve a national fraud scheme in just one single suit. Maybe it is wrong to bring such a "national" suit under a single state's fraud law in a single state court. But it's better than to have no one suit at all.

Yes, I understand CAFA if the purpose is to deregulate fraud. At least it's a rational reason (for those who commit it). But it will lead to more not less litigation. What is the point? Sometimes I think the Right simply dislikes the rationality of class actions. It's too sensible for them. Why have just one plaintiff suing? Why not have 50,000 people sue? Then we will all drive each other nuts. It will be like talk radio. Maybe the logic is: The more free-floating anger there is in this country, the better it is for a party that feeds upon rage.

Still, it is nuts to knock out these national class actions—to have 50,000 sue instead of one. But it's not just more litigation; there are more arbitrary outcomes. For the same fraudulent scheme, some win, some lose. Now there's even more rage. The domestic gross output of resentment goes up.

Of course I am speaking theoretically. If we stop a national class action of 50,000 people, there surely will not be 50,000 suits. But under CAFA, there could be five or six or maybe forty or more "state" class actions for what is but a single fraudulent scheme. It's still the same result. Some win. Some lose. There is no single Rule of Law. It leads to more people feeling violated.

Let's take fifty sets of depositions in each of the fifty states. Let's have fifty rounds of discovery. Let's multiply the legal costs by fifty. Let's have fifty different legal systems come up with fifty different results.

I understand why business wants to deregulate fraud. But they can't get rid of class actions completely. For one thing, it's really the trade-off for a weak regulatory state. We use bounty hunters here. Get rid of class actions, and there is no Rule of Law, at least with respect to fraud. And that is something bad for business. Get rid of all this law, and it's difficult to plan. "Is my rival going to cheat? What really are the rules?" It's true that in France and other countries they don't need class actions to perform this kind of stabilizing function. They have strong states instead. But without class actions in the United States, we would have chaos until the government stepped in. On the whole, business is far better off dealing with lawyers who try to certify classes than with government officials or prosecutors who represent the public. With class actions, the business defendants have real leverage over the plaintiff lawyers. "Your Honor, so-and-so should not represent the class. They lie. They cheat. They're scoundrels. They won't do a good job." It's much harder to say these things about a regulatory agency.

And if a company has to face some class actions, in the state courts anyway, why not have it just be one? In 2006, according to a survey reported on the front page of the *Financial Times*, the top 1,000 corporations spent over $56 billion on legal fees for "outside" (not in-house) counsel. That's up a whopping 20 percent from the year before. The cry went up: "It's because there is more regulation." That may be true, but it's also because there is more deregulation. They knock down national class actions and end up with more state by state class actions than before. The more we limit class actions, the more rage there is, and the harder it is to bring an end to litigation.

The other day I got a call from Ed who had a faulty pacemaker from Guidant put in his chest. The pacemakers blow fuses, so they had to have a "recall." But this is not like a recall of a Ford. During the operation, Ed got pneumonia and almost died. When he was strong enough to open the mail, some plaintiff class action lawyer was soliciting him to join a suit.

"No," he said to me. "I want to bring my own suit. I want you to do it."

"Me?"

"I want you to do it. I want to control my own suit."

"But that's the whole point of these class actions. Why don't you let somebody else have the aggravation?"

It took me a while to talk him out of bringing his own suit. That's just what the right wants, isn't it? It wants 10,000 heart patients with bad tickers bringing their own suits. Let them stress out in depositions. Let's make them even sicker. Let's have them, one by one, deal with the attacks on their character: "Isn't it true you had a cigarette?" "As you sit here now, do you recall whether you have ever had a Big Mac at McDonald's?"

I tried to suggest to Ed: Think of your ticker. That's what class actions are for. Let somebody else sue.

It's also true that as the economy becomes more global it is hard to resolve cases without at least a national class action. Here I would like to tell the story of when I brought a coupon suit.

Yes, I brought one of the notorious coupon suits, where the recovery was so small to each individual customer that they only got coupons as a result. And here one might accuse me: "You aren't cutting down litigation, you're adding to it. You're bringing a suit that no one person individually would bring."

It's true. What do members of the class get? Very little, in terms of cash. Yes, they can even end up with mere coupons— for example, $20 off the next time they deal with the company that defrauded.

A friend once said to me: "You'd never do that kind of suit, would you? You'd never bring a coupon case."

He thinks I'm an idealist, a crusader. And he has his own crusade, to get the lawyers who bring these cases. "It's my mission," he said, "to go after lawyers who bring these kinds of cases."

I blushed. "Bill," I said, "I've got to confess—I did a coupon case."

His eyes widened. It's as if I had said: "Behold, I am Satan." He seemed to draw his breath.

"And I'll never do it again," I said. For one thing I can't, not since CAFA became law. We brought a "national" class action in a state under a single state fraud law. Even though twenty-five or thirty other states have very similar laws, technically, it is one state's law applied to a fraud scheme that involved fifty states. So I did just what CAFA tried to stop.

Why not? It was fraud. And without a single class action, there would have been no way to resolve it.

Our little firm took the case, with our co-counsel Rob and Scott. We had a tip-off about an add-on that a company was slipping in the final sales price. Let's call the company Foreign Fun. It sells a vacation-type service, which I will not name. The scheme was this: they give the "base" price, without the foreign sales tax. Then when the final bill comes, they add on the foreign sales tax, the "VAT."

What's the fraud? There is no foreign sales tax. France or
Italy can't tax a sale by an American company (Foreign Fun)
to an American citizen (you) in America. Remember that
the next time you pay a foreign sales tax on a transaction that
takes place entirely in the United States. Even if you live in
Manhattan, you're still an American, dealing with an American company.

So in our own state court, Illinois, we sued Foreign Fun, for
charging these fake VATs in all fifty of the U.S. states. That's
just what Bush's CAFA was set up to stop. But there is no federal consumer law under which we can sue. And if we did not
sue for a national class, we would have to bring fifty separate
class actions in our fifty separate states. Isn't that crazy? We
need fifty more classes to certify, fifty more class representatives to be deposed, fifty hotels in which we'd have to spend
the nights, fifty more sets of files to rifle through. Why not
one national class action instead of multiplying the agony
fifty times?

"But Foreign Fun isn't based in Illinois." That's right. Neither is Wal-Mart. But these companies aren't really the citizens
of any state. That's a pious fiction. Technically, Foreign Fun
was in state M, a half-continent away. But, in fact, it did more
business in Illinois than it did in state M.

Along with Foreign Fun, we sued two other companies that
were doing the same thing as Foreign Fun. These two competitors were also operating in all fifty states. Indeed, they were
global. One was British-owned, the other German-owned. No,
Foreign Fun was not based in Illinois. But it was not based any-
where, really, though it had an office in state M. But to fight us,
they brought in a law firm not from state M but from state F—
well, I might as well just say Florida. Why would Foreign Fun
in state M go to a firm in Miami, Florida, to handle a case in
Chicago, Illinois? I don't know. It doesn't make any difference:

that's my point. It's a global economy. In a few years, in Chicago, I may be fighting over a payday loan in state court with lawyers flying in from London.

But I doubt that Foreign Fun in state M was even our real opponent. It was their insurance company in New York. They're the ones who went to get the lawyers in Florida. (Are you following all this?)

"Okay," you say, "but in the end, you're using the law of just one little state, Illinois, to get a scheme that's nationwide! Why pick out just one state's law? It's not fair!"

Of course it's fair. Fraud is fraud, isn't it? Anyway, it isn't "one little state." Yes, it's an Illinois law, but on consumer fraud Illinois has a uniform model law that most of the states have adopted. The Illinois Consumer Fraud and Deceptive Practices Act is the same model law, more or less, as the uniform model law enacted in Connecticut and many other states. The biggest difference from one uniform model law to the other is that ours has the word "Illinois" and theirs has the word "Connecticut." These "model" laws came out of the 1940s and 1950s, when law professors would draft them and there was a fashion for thinking rationally and uniformly. Most states cheerfully adopted the "model" laws. Now, in our time, it would never happen: we put a premium on disparity and arbitrariness. But, one may ask, why did they not just have one big national law? It's a fair question. But in the 1940s and 1950s we still lived in a time of largely local markets. Nothing like a website or 800 number could even be imagined. It was regarded as sensible and more practical to have uniform model laws state by state, not so the laws could facilitate national class actions, since they would have made no sense at the time, but to ensure a uniform law, as they literally said. Now this kind of impulse to uniformity and rationality is exhausted. The legal Dark Ages are upon us.

The one big national consumer law we do have comes from Woodrow Wilson: the Fair Trade Commission Act. It is just like the model state law, except that private consumers have no standing. Only the FTC can sue. Perhaps in Wilson's time, no one imagined that "private" consumers had the resources to go to court to stop nationwide fraud. Maybe the premise in 1914 was that in a largely local economy, the only such nationwide fraud would involve the railroads or the Standard Oil Trust— big octopus things that no local people could take on. There was nothing like, well, Foreign Fun.

So Foreign Fun runs free. One federal agency like the FTC is not set up to catch all the fraud. It has to let be. But when we sued, Foreign Fun, or their New York insurance company, or their law firm in Miami, or all three of them, plus the two other companies, came flying in here to express shock that we'd try to apply the law of Illinois outside of Illinois. Of course, the law firm meters began ticking. There were at least four separate firms. I say "at least" because Foreign Fun and the two other defendant companies launched major lawsuits against their respective New York insurance companies as to how much (if any) insurance coverage each defendant would receive. These separate insurance cases were in federal court, where we could not sue! To our amazement, two of these cases went up to the U.S. Court of Appeals for the Seventh Circuit over the same issue, that is, how much the New York insurers had to cover the fraud we were alleging in state court. Naturally, even though it was the same issue, the two cases came out in entirely different ways.

Meanwhile, while they were litigating insurance coverage in federal court, our little firm and our little co-counsel firm were floundering to get a national class action in the state court in Illinois. We tried one argument, then another. We spent two or three lifetimes writing briefs, and getting briefs, that filled two or three bins.

Foreign Fun had terrific lawyers, especially the local counsel in Chicago. I wanted to give up. I kept trying to persuade my co-counsel to quit. "I can't go on." But in the end, they wanted to settle too.

Wait, my liberal friends say—they beat you. Why would they want to settle? Yes, it's a puzzle to them why little liberal types like me even keep practicing law. "Isn't the law against you?" Yes. "Aren't the corporate firms too strong for you?" Yes. "Isn't it getting worse every day?" Yes.

Then why do you go on?

It's true enough: the courts, the firms, can crush us now, and often do. But in this case, even if we had no class, not even in Illinois, and even if in the end we were down to representing a single consumer, with a $25 claim, the fact is, we could still take the deposition of Mr. Foreign Fun, the CEO.

Believe me, Mr. Foreign Fun did not want us to take his deposition—to ask him, under oath, why he was charging a VAT.

Anyway, that's why we go on practicing law.

But the case was hard to settle. What was the sticking point?

Foreign Fun would settle only if it was a national class action. While the lawyers in Miami had spent two years fighting against a national class action, it turns out that that was their principal demand on us. "What? You're joking." I would not joke. Foreign Fun, which ran up huge costs to fight a national class action, wanted one thing above all: a national class action.

And typically the defendant fighting a national class action wants a national class action as much as, or more than, the plaintiffs do. The reason: to end the litigation. "We don't want to be dealing with fifty suits, do we?" From a business point of view, it's crazy not to have a national class action. They want to know the bottom line.

So a reader may reasonably say: "Wait. They fight what they want? I'm not getting this." Well, no one gets it. I used to think: "I have a warped view as a lawyer for the plaintiffs, and it actually makes sense for them to fight it." But the other day I was before a very experienced judge, an expert in complex litigation and class actions and the author of several articles on class actions. He shook his head: "I don't understand why they fight class actions."

Not only that: the CEOs whooped and shouted and high-fived each other when they got Congress to pass CAFA. But the probable success of insulating themselves from civil fraud liability in my rinky-dink little case is that several of these CEOs will end up one day in a federal prison instead. Somebody in one of the fifty state class actions will depose him under oath. Or maybe no one will sue. The fraud will just go on until one day a U.S. attorney somewhere will decide to prosecute. I could write a book about it all, and call it *The Death of Common Sense,* except that someone has already used that title.

There is still one taunt that can be flung at me: "In the end you just got crappy little coupons for the class members. You walked away with the only money in the case." That's true. As I say, the lawyers on the other side were tough. And on appeal, they could have beaten us, not just on the national class issue but maybe on other procedural points too. It's pretty hostile in these appellate courts, as I will explain below. And they probably had more high cards than we did.

Or maybe they didn't, and I'm easy to bluff. Maybe we should have held out for cash to the class, since the coupon just meant they got $25 off the "base price" the next time the coupon-holder called up Foreign Fun.

On the other hand, did $25 in cash really matter to the affluent thousands who were the customers of Foreign Fun? That's what they spend on a Starbucks. (Of course, it was a huge amount of money every year to Foreign Fun.)

Anyway, we did coupons.

Still, I blushed when we sent out the notices to the class. People phoned or wrote: "You mean I'm only getting this coupon?" Or: "Why did you pick on this fine business?" Or: "What did you accomplish except to get your stupid fees? I'm so sick of you lawyers."

What did you accomplish? Hey, we stopped the fraud! This is a suit that would never be brought except as a class action, partly to get our fees and partly to scare them into settling. Anyway, that's the point: the fraud is over. But for this suit, it would have gone on and on. The FTC would not have cared.

But we could never bring a suit like this now. We'd have to file in fifty state courts. Or we would be removed to federal court. The business defendants would then argue that the federal court would have to apply "state" law, state by state, and certify fifty subclasses. "Your Honor," they say, "that's so unmanageable. You can't have fifty subclasses, based on fifty different laws." Many judges will agree:

"You're right, Counsel. I can't apply fifty laws to fifty subclasses."

Can't the case go on for a handful? Sure, but then no one will want to settle. (Remember, to settle, business wants a national class.) And the fraud will go on and on until it gets bigger, on the scale of an Enron, and there's a criminal prosecution.

If this is the worst domestic law that comes out of Bush's second term, I suppose we should count ourselves lucky. I try to remember that what Congress did to me and the other class action lawyers is not nearly as bad as what they did to the detainees.

Perhaps I should blush that I'm arguing for a big national fraud type tort suit. Well, I don't. I'm not against torts! What I'm against is anything that makes the legal system more fragmentary, less uniform, or just plain crazy and unfair. That's why we should amend the Federal Trade Commission Act and let U.S. citizens sue under a federal consumer fraud law, in federal court, in nationwide suits. That would have made vastly more sense than bashing class actions as we did with CAFA. Believe me, I can understand the case for CAFA, for stopping nationwide class actions in the state courts. If I were a big business operating nationwide, some state courts would scare me. In some of these little Sleepy Hollow hellholes, I'd worry that my little big business would get mugged.

But, of course, the CEOs don't want national class actions in federal court, either. Indeed, if they had a choice, they'd rather be in state court with fifty fragmented class actions. Even better, they'd like to go up against one plaintiff, one little old $25 case at a time.

Yet by bashing class actions, business adds to the cost of litigation. As in the case of Foreign Fun, it is only through class actions that businesses with big legal problems can put it all behind them. There's no way to dispose of a fraud or a scandal and move on. If there is no class action, there may be some other kind of closure—perhaps a criminal prosecution. Ask Jeffrey Skilling of Enron. There are worse things than being sued in a mere civil case for fraud.

Stop the nationwide class action from wrapping up cases, and the litigation in America is never going to stop.

CHAPTER 7

Why Litigation Costs Are Going Up

I sympathize with business. Litigation costs are going up right now. But why don't they look at what their lawyers charge them?

A good friend of mine is in manufacturing. "You talk to people in industry, and their big complaint is lawyers." Every time a worker gets hurt, the guy sues everyone in sight. Now, as a union-side lawyer I am tempted to reply: "Well, since these CEOs got rid of unions, they only have to deal with lawyers. OK, they don't like it. But look at the money they save now that they get to cut off health insurance for retirees, cancel the old pension plans, and jack up their own salaries with no union there to chide them." It seems a small price to deal with a plaintiff lawyer like me.

But business has a point, and it's not so easily answered by the left. Litigation costs are going up. It's easy to say, "Our side is not to blame." By "our side" I mean not just the plaintiffs or the plaintiff lawyers but the juries, the jury verdicts, the people's democracy at work.

I suppose one would expect me to say: "Juries are not to blame." But I really think it's true. Consider just one area, medical malpractice. The price of health care is rising much faster than the verdict in any good study of jury awards I have seen. One might even argue that if the price of health care is rising faster than jury awards, the juries are giving doctors an incentive to commit medical error. At any rate, even a study by the General Accounting Office authorized by a Republican Congress decided in 2003 that no big rise in jury verdicts are to blame.

But let's consider jury verdicts in general. Aren't there blockbuster verdicts that could wreck whole companies and lead to layoffs of workers?

Okay, I admit it—there are some excessive verdicts: wild blockbuster verdicts, of $10 billion or more, which could shatter some companies. In the 2004 campaign Bush and Cheney made a big issue of these blockbuster verdicts. Bush liked to finger a single county, Madison County, in my own state of Illinois. Indeed, he so demonized this one county that it seemed like part of the axis of evil, a foreign country like North Korea or Iran.

Well, I share a bit of Bush's grudge against Madison County, Illinois. They aren't helping my life. As I will explain, these blockbuster verdicts rile up the big CEOs. Then they pour huge amounts of cash into judicial races, so they can put in rightwing Supreme Court justices to toss the verdicts out. Then, once business's justices are in, they now go on to do harm in my areas of the law, labor, and the like. It's the liberals who ought to oppose the blockbuster verdicts even more than Bush does. The blowback from the judges that the CEOs elect ends up hurting a whole series of good causes.

Still, it's hard for me to hate Madison County, despite all the harm it's been doing to the courts. There must be a book or movie here: *The Juries of Madison County,* or *The County*

Mouse that Roared. I like to imagine that it all started when they lost a bid for a penitentiary and had to figure out a new way to come up with jobs, or the kids would start leaving town. Then one of the elders of Madison County gets an idea: "Why don't we all just start giving out verdicts in billions? Then all the plaintiff lawyers will come to sue." "But won't Bush get mad at us?" "We have to take care of our families." So that's just what they do. Soon, from all over the country, big plaintiff and defendant law firms are flying in on private jets. Of course they want Starbucks, bistros, the best hotels. Soon the young people of Madison County are making big money as chefs.

OK, I'm kidding: I'm sure that isn't how it happened.

At any rate, I'm against blockbuster verdicts out of obscure little counties, or any jury handing out awards so high that they lay waste to institutions. Still, there are very few of these verdicts, and few of them last for long. Let's take the two big Madison County verdicts, one for $10 billion against Philip Morris and a lesser $1.05 billion against State Farm. Both of them: poof, up in smoke. The higher court tossed them out. So it is with many blockbuster verdicts that seem at first to be the end of companies.

I have a friend, an economist, who wrote a paper listing and excoriating these verdicts for all the carnage they would do. But even he admitted they were few: he listed about ten, and a year or two later a good number of them were toast. Our judicial system is well set up to reduce blockbuster verdicts. The laity fails to get this. In my first year of law school, we spent a whole class of Civil Procedure on the concept of "remittitur," by which a trial judge can reduce a verdict, yes, even or especially a verdict in the billions. If the trial judge lacks the nerve, the appellate judges pull the plug. Then there is the state supreme court. Remember, the higher up in state court, the more likely the judges are to be Republicans. Even if they are Democrats, they are more cautious. Since it can cost up to $4 million to run for high court, and the money has to come from somewhere, it is a genuine judicial concern for the fortunes of big business.

In Illinois, for example, after Philip Morris and State Farm were hit with these billion-dollar verdicts, both companies threw themselves into our state judicial elections. These big verdicts get their attention. According to Common Cause and other groups, both companies directly or indirectly gave big sums to Justice Lloyd Karmeier, running for election to the Illinois Supreme Court. In the case of State Farm, the allegation was that State Farm employees contributed the money, a sum supposedly over $350,000. When Karmeier won—he actually raised a total of $4.5 million—he sat on the appeals of the two blockbuster verdicts. Whatever the appearance of it, he voted to reverse. I was one of the lawyers who signed a letter protesting his participation in these cases. But nothing came of the letter, and the verdicts went away.

As I noted, there is one lasting effect: once on the court, these very pro-business judges will decide the fate of other liberal causes. With no Madison County, we might have a more progressive court.

Besides, progressives have a second, bigger reason to be against the rare or oddball blockbuster verdict. When a big oddball verdict pops out, other jurors may react by cutting back normal bread-and-butter verdicts. Jurors start to panic. "My insurance will go up!" The other day, my friend M., a sensible businesswoman, came by the office. Across the street, in Circuit Court, she had just escaped being picked for jury duty. "This morning," she said, "someone in our jury pool asked the judge, 'Is there any limit to what we can award?' "

She paused. "You know what the judge said to her? He said, 'There are no limits!' "

Though way on the left, she's also a CPA. She rolled her eyes: " 'There are no limits!' "

"Well, there *are* limits," I snapped. "It has to be reasonable. Reasonableness is a limit." After all, that's why judges can reduce verdicts. But my riff on "remittitur" did not reassure her. And I can see why jurors panic. They see the soaring insurance rates. "My God," they think, "we've got to stop it." Wages are stagnating. Health care costs go up.

But their restraint has had no effect so far. Or so it seems from the one area of tort law which has received the most study: medical malpractice. Let me try out again the argument that if juries hold back in medical malpractice, and medical error goes unpunished, it could lead to more error and ultimately higher rates.

"That's impossible," some will say.

Well, I can't prove it.

Here's how it could happen: while medical malpractice studies are highly political and have to be approached with caution, it seems the jury verdicts in this area, on the whole, have been stable in recent years, especially if adjusted for inflation. Or so it seems from the more neutral studies, like the GAO's report in 2003. The liberal groups argue convincingly to me that the net malpractice claims paid out by insurance companies stayed more or less the same in recent years.

At the same time, everyone knows that medical prices have shot up remarkably. The price of health care, the cost of premiums, the cost of malpractice insurance, all of them have soared. In September 2006 the Kaiser Family Foundation issued a report that shows that over the last five years inflation generally has gone up 18 percent but the cost that people pay for health care has gone up by an astounding 84 percent! If jury verdicts are low as trillions of dollars are gushing into health care, it may be that juries are tacitly encouraging medical error, or at least giving insufficient incentive for doctors to root it out. Of course one could reply, sensibly: "But the cost of malpractice insurance is going up like crazy. Wouldn't that create an incentive?" No, it wouldn't, if cutting down medical error in and of itself had no effect. If the rates go up anyway, and if there is no connection to actual medical error, we may have a situation where juries are letting error go unpunished and there is not much incentive to improve things. But is there any evidence that serious medical error is being tolerated by cowardly juries?

Yes, there is fairly disturbing evidence.

In the May 2006 issue, the *New England Journal of Medicine* published the best study I could find of medical malpractice awards. It was based on a Harvard School of Public Health study of 1,452 "closed" medical malpractice claims. According to the study, in one out of six cases, there was both "serious injury" and "serious medical error" but the jury awarded nothing, not a dime. Imagine how the plaintiff's lawyer feels: maybe five years of work, a great case, serious medical negligence, and not a single cent for his client. No wonder John Edwards got out of trial work. Indeed, the study made it clear that juries are hostile. According to the Harvard team, patients "rarely won damages at trial, prevailing in only 21 percent of verdicts as compared with 61 percent of claims resolved out of court." As to frivolous awards in favor of plaintiffs, the study found next to zero. Where there was no "serious injury" or no "serious medical error," a patient rarely got anything, even in settlement.

The next time you're a patient, you may see the result of this jury restraint. How many nurses do you see on the floor? When hospitals cut back on nurses, medical error goes up. So does the mortality rate. Right before your eyes, though, you can see the hospitals cutting back. Obviously, they aren't worried as to what juries are going to do.

Still, there is no similar study for jury verdicts generally. And there is no doubt that litigation costs are going up. What's the explanation?

First, there are a lot more cases. I tried to give reasons for why expensive tort-type cases are going up. But it's not just tort. The National Center for State Courts did a count in twenty-five states. It claims that the rise in litigation comes not in tort cases but in contract. One may ask: then are we really moving from tort to contract? We certainly are, in employment law and many other areas. But these new, expensive tort-type claims (civil rights, whistle-blowing) are not what the NCSC is counting as tort. They are counting the old-fashioned personal-injury type of case. They are counting fender-benders and car wrecks, not the new type torts with big firms and hugely expensive discovery. And if the NCSC did a breakdown of the new "contract" cases, I bet a million dollars that the increase is almost entirely in "collection" cases. These are not contested lawsuits, but cookie-cutter default judgments, which are entered against the most wretched of their customers. In other words, it is U.S. business that is blowing up its own litigation costs as it chases after desperate single moms and others too poor to fight back. If U.S. business has higher legal costs, it's partly because it has to sue so many people it's driven into debt.

Second, the "administrative cost" of each suit is going up. In medical malpractice, it's not higher jury awards but the "administrative" cost that is the problem. The *New England Journal* study was emphatic: "The overhead costs of malpractice litigation are exorbitant." For every dollar in compensation that is awarded, 54 cents goes for administrative cost.

Yes, we're paying more for lawyers. I'm sure the insurance companies are greedy. But they do have to pay for lawyers. In the *Financial Times* story of January 2, 2007, the claim was that legal fees to outside counsel paid by the Fortune 1000 have gone up 20 percent in just one year. Twenty percent! Even I have trouble believing that. Yes, plaintiff lawyers like me bring these suits. Yes, I am responsible. But I get my take from the money going to my clients. I am not charging, like the big firms, up to $800 or more an hour. I don't force the other side to take a ridiculous number of depositions, or hold poor high school grads hostage while blue-chip lawyers work them over. Of course the bills that my opponents charge to their clients are preposterous. But so far as I can tell, the CEOs of America are happy to pay. If they pay excessive amounts to top lawyers, the lawyers will be happy to defend their excessive salaries. If litigation costs are rising, it is in part because the plutocracy is throwing a party.

Yes, I think I can say so from personal experience. Every day I see the bizarre new ways the lawyers on the other side spend money on themselves. Now that I think about it, I can see why the bills go up 20 percent a year. "Oh, he's exaggerating," many a reader will say. Let me give a small example.

We have a big case against certain corporate directors who cut off benefits to their workers—something they would never attempt in Europe or Japan. We wanted to drop one of the directors who had tried to stay out of the scheme. When we gave notice of a routine motion to drop him, one of the big New York firms in the case objected.

"You can't serve us by fax," they said. They were flying out from New York the next day to Chicago to object that we had used a fax to send the motion. Their argument was: at the out-set of the case, they had never sent in the usual form consent-ing to be served by fax.

Now there is such a rule, but it came in the 1980s when fax machines were novelties. This is the twenty-first century, and everyone's on e-mail. And, in fact, they had been accepting fax copies up to now. Aha, but they had not formally consented! So that's why the New York firms were flying out. In fact, they were presenting an emergency motion.

That was the reason—they got a fax? Yes, that was the reason.

"I don't believe it," I said to Carol, our associate.

But I *did* believe it: that's what I find hard to believe. And not only did they fly out from New York, but they stayed in nice downtown Loop hotels. Of course they all went out to dinner on their corporate clients.

The next morning, when they argued about the fax, the judge stared at them in disbelief. That's why they filed an emergency motion?

Yes.

There is a delicious moment when the other side realizes from the judge's look that maybe this time they have gone too far. They began to back track: "Of course, as your Honor wishes . . . ," etc.

He made clear he never wanted this done in his courtroom again. Well, we won one! We can high-five each other.

Six firms showed up to litigate whether one of them had an obligation to consent to service of a routine motion by a fax.

As I walked back, I tried to figure out the cost of the whole proceeding. The lawyers (or the New York ones) bill at $800 or more an hour. I know because a former college roommate of mine is in the firm. I tried to add the cost of the dinners, the hotel rooms, the flights. All of it spent to decide whether they had to read a pristine elegant copy from a superb million-dollar fax machine at a blue-chip firm, or whether they could read a photocopy by overnight mail. For all the money that was blown on this stupid little motion, I could have rented a farmhouse in Tuscany and read D.H. Lawrence for a year.

But here's what really galled me. The lead plaintiff is dying. He may not last the case. And the more these lawyers run up the bills, the less money there is in the pot to settle. That's because the insurance policy is what we lawyers call a "self-cannibalizing policy." It eats itself. Let's say the policy on the directors is worth $20 million. The lawyers for the defendants are drawing that money down, at the rate of $800 an hour.

Soon, as they fly out to argue over service by fax, it's $19 million, then $18 million, then $17 million. *That's the money for the workers!* And the more it drops, the harder it is to settle within the policy limits.

"It's like in *Bleak House*," someone may say. "You know, the lawyers eat up the estate, and then there's nothing left."

Well, it's not like *Bleak House*, because in the Dickens novel, all the other lawyers are getting something, while I'm without a dime. I'm in court and fuming over a fax, and before my eyes, I can see this big pot of money cannibalizing itself.

Bon appetit—and I'm getting acid reflux.

As I kept walking I realized how the tort system is now an engine of inequality. In law school I learned that the tort system is a form of redistribution: the railroads are the great example.

Let's say a train hits me. "Hey, we were negligent, we hit you, but look, we'll pay you off." It's a way of redistributing from the deep pocket to the empty one, taking from the rich and giving to the poor.

But when I'm in court and the lawyers on the other side are charging $800 or more an hour to argue over a fax in a way they would blush to do in kindergarten, I realize that the money is going the other way. A tort case is now often a way of redistributing from the little people at the bottom to the big people at the top.

Think of the cases where plaintiffs are disabled or paralyzed or in a coma because a hospital cut back on nurses or a railroad is working engineers around the clock. Sometimes the plaintiffs get nothing. Yet the lawyers could be making $800 an hour, for hours where they fly out from New York to quibble about a fax.

And the more people sue, the richer they get. The more I bring suits, the richer I make them. When I read how lawyers make these sums, even breaking $1,000 an hour, I feel sorry for the businesses that pay them.

But aren't I part of the problem? The more suits I bring, the more income in this country is redistributed to the top. The more we sue over looting of pension funds or just plain old-fashioned medical error, the more the money flows to people at the top—to law firms, to "experts," to the insurance companies.

That's how it works in a plutocracy. The more we sue the rich, the richer the rich get. And the poor just end up "self-cannibalizing" themselves.

CHAPTER 8

How Attacking Litigation Is Increasing Litigation

S till, business hates to be sued. Even if we lose or the juries are getting worse, we can still impose big litigation costs. We can still take their depositions under oath. "That's what they hate," a corporate lawyer friend of mine said. So business has two ways to hold down litigation.

The first: to get you and me, whether we're consumers or employees, to sign a release waiving all our rights to sue them, no matter how much they defraud us. Later, I'll discuss the problem: how can we release them if we don't know what they did to us?

The second way is better for them: to get us to arbitrate any dispute, not with a neutral arbitrator, but with one of their people. Arbitration is much, much better, especially for consumer cases. In a way, it's set up so business can sue us, but we can't sue them. Perhaps it will take the place of courts.

But at the moment, all these ways of attacking litigation are increasing litigation. Let's take them one by one.

Releases

If you do a Lexis printout of every case in which I have filed an appearance, you might think that all I do as a lawyer is fight about releases. A release is the boilerplate at the end of a consumer contract or a worker buyout agreement.

I hereby release Bank Big One, and its assigns, and parents, subsidiaries, agents, principals, directors and next of kin from any liability to me for any violation by Bank Big One of my rights under any federal or state law of any kind ever passed by legislative body, as well as any and all harm to me from any act of war, or fraudulent act, or negligence, or intentional assault against me, or any waterboarding or violation of the Geneva Convention, or any other deprivation of my rights, and I promise to give up my right to habeas corpus and my right to sue in any court. Nonetheless, if I sue, then Bank Big One is authorized by me to obtain a judgment against me for all its legal fees without any notice to me and to collect an additional liquidated penalty in the sum of $3,000,000, unless Bank Big One in its sole discretion determines it should be twenty times as much.

That's a release. You may have signed one, often without knowing it, since you may "agree" or "sign" it by the very act of using a credit card.

In labor law, I see them all the time. Any time there is a buyout or a layoff, there's a release: "I release you from any act of fraud even if I don't know what it is." So far I have had reasonably good luck in breaking the release. It is still the law that when I release my right to sue, it has to be a "knowing and voluntary" act. If I release you from liability for cheating me in the very contract I'm signing, that doesn't make a lot of sense, does it?

Well, that's the rule. Or I guess it's the rule. I hope it's the rule. But after thirty years of fighting over the validity of these releases, I still have to admit to clients that I don't know if this release will hold up in court or not.

My friend Alan does consumer law for the poor in Legal Services, and he's the best consumer lawyer in the city. "I keep breaking them" he told me, "but then they keep drafting these releases better and better." It's true—but then our side keeps coming up with new ways to break them, that is, to get a judge to throw them out and let us sue Bank Big One for fraud our clients didn't know about.

One good way to break a release is "lack of mutuality." The problem for business is that while they complain about litigation, they love to litigate—against their customers. "We hate litigation" they say. And they do—when we sue them. But they want to sue us. They *have* to sue us. We're all in debt. We can't afford these things we're buying.

So business is always trying to draft releases or try other devices that let them go on suing us but stop us from suing them. Yet there is a rule that releases should be mutual. Let's say I go to Wal-Mart and buy an "original" painting by Caravaggio. I sign a release waiving my right to sue: "I promise not to sue if it turns out that this Caravaggio was really painted by an employee working off the clock."

Is that valid? No!

A release has to be mutual. It's not "mutual" if Wal-Mart can sue me for paying in Monopoly money but I can't sue them because the original Caravaggio was painted by an employee working off the clock.

Here's a case we have. The employer says: "You've been with us for years. But we have to cut the workforce. It's too bad. But we'll give you some severance pay if you give up your right to be recalled—and you should, because this business isn't coming back."

So people sign. They give up their rights to recall. They resign from the union. They've lost these great jobs at $22 an hour. There's no reason to hang on. They sign releases that say, in effect, "Thanks for the severance pay, and of course we give up all our rights to sue, and if we dare to break this agreement, you can sue us and recover all your legal fees in defending any case we bring."

As soon as they sign, the company begins rehiring, not older employees but young kids, at $11 an hour.

Of course, the old-timers are outraged: "They lied to us!"

"But you signed a release!"

But it can't be valid, can it? I hope not. Now that we have sued, the employer's law firm keeps sending us letters: "Now you owe us $250,000. And if you go on taking depositions of our managers, it will get even higher." And so on. Our clients are in a rage. But they're also terrified.

And I'm terrified—even though I'm in a rage. ("How can they do this?")

Maybe this case here will end up shattering us and our clients, but win or lose, the fight over the release, by itself, has doubled, or perhaps trebled, or even quadrupled, the cost of this litigation. It's standard now. In our country, a good part of the fraud litigation is now about the validity of the release. It seems that at every income level, whether it's a widow in a pay-day loan store or a trader in futures joining the East Bank Club, we all sign releases.

Yes, even at the top, they have to sign away their right to sue.

My friend L is sending her two little girls to a blue-chip private school, a Baby Bennington College Prep. She pays a mint. The other day Baby Bennington sends a letter: Will Ms. L release Baby Bennington from all liability if the little boys at the school use the school computers to sexually harass her daughters?

The lawyers want it: Baby Bennington can't be liable.

L is furious. She won't sign.

Baby Bennington says: "But we can't be the insurers of your daughter."

"Why not?"

"You have to sign the release."

"No. I expect you to control the kids."

And so it stands. But L is still astonished: "Can you believe that parents have signed this?"

Sure, and in fact, when I told this story to a friend—a businessman with two daughters—he was irked with L and me.

"I'm on the school's side. I'd sign that release. You can't be absolute insurers against that kind of thing!"

Now I'm irked. "No one's talking about making them 'absolute insurers.' This isn't a release from strict liability, I mean, like in a case where they were storing, oh, dynamite next to your house. You're releasing them from *any* liability, even for like, oh, using ordinary common sense. It's as if, well, they could jump on these girls in front of the teachers, and heck, they could laugh, and applaud and not do a damn thing. *That's what you're signing.*"

Oh well. Anyway, I'm on L's side.

The bad thing is, the more that companies and banks and schools and hospitals can get us all to sign releases, the worse they will behave. There's no "cost." We will pay the costs. The economy will. Yet all over the country people are signing releases, releasing companies from acts of fraud, releasing them from ordinary due care.

And of course the courts are full of cases of people fighting over releases. It's led both to more corporate recklessness and higher litigation costs. Besides, I'm sick of litigating them. I'd rather get to the merits of the case.

By the way, I'm strongly in favor of releases when people

know what they're releasing. I depend for my living on settling cases, and there wouldn't be any settlement if there wasn't a release.

Though it's not the same point, there is a growing view on the right that business has a First Amendment right to lie to people. Or at least that it is illegal, and maybe even unconstitutional, for government to pass a law prohibiting or regulating fraud. I know, it sounds incredible. I admit, this legal movement is still in its infancy. But already some law professors on the right, like Charles Fried of Harvard, argue that this is one of the great legacies of the Rehnquist court. It's the principle of business free speech. It starts with innocent advertising and it can end up with the right to deceive. In one ERISA case, *Varity Corp. v. Howe et al.* (1996), workers sued a business for lying to them to take an illusory pension-type benefit. To defend its right to mislead the workers, the company brought in the country's greatest First Amendment lawyer, Floyd Abrams. He didn't have to argue the First Amendment right to lie. His very presence made the point.

Thank God, his client lost—but only by 5 to 4. With the new Court, he'd probably win the case today.

And if there is a right to lie, then I'll never break these releases. But why worry about releases? Arbitration clauses are spreading. That's even bigger trouble for our side.

Arbitration clauses

You've signed one. Check your credit card agreement. I bet it says: "I agree that any dispute or claim either Bank Big One or I have will be decided not in a court but in a private arbitration." Maybe it will name the arbitration company. The best known is the National Arbitration Forum, in Minneapolis. (Some might call it the National Arbitration Factory.) No, you don't "release" anything but the right to go to court. But Bank Big One picks the arbitrator: they "pay" the Forum, or the Factory.

"Just five years ago," my friend Alan says, "I saw arbitration clauses in 10 percent of the consumer contracts here. Now it's up to 80 percent."

Soon it will be 100 percent: they are in contracts for payday loans, for auto loans, for nursing home care, and, of course, for credit cards. Soon there will be no right to sue, just to arbitrate. Think of it—business will have privatized the entire world of litigation.

And it's their arbitrator, not yours. Bank Big One pays. It's their handpicked guy who decides.

What are your chances of winning? You're not paying the guy. You're not the repeat player. Who do you think is going to win? Well, since it's all private and out of court, the whole process is secret. No one knows the total record. But a few years ago, there was a suit challenging First USA for using these mass arbitrations. There was enough pretrial disclosure to allow a peek inside the process.

First USA won *more than 99 percent* of the arbitrations. It won 99.6 percent of the time. There is a box score in the March 1, 2000, *Washington Post.* Here's the total for just a two-year period.

Victories by First USA: 19,618
Victories by customers: 87

Yet how can I attack arbitrations? In Chapter 1, I was nostalgic for old-fashioned union-management arbitration. But those arbitrators were neutral since both sides appointed and paid for them. In the old days, they were gray-haired old men, retired law professors, who cast their first vote for Franklin Roosevelt, or maybe even Norman Thomas. Even so, they had to keep both sides happy if they wanted to keep working.

But these arbitrators aren't neutral. They aren't fair. They make pitches to Bank Big One and their ilk: "Let us arbitrate for you. We promise to lower your litigation costs."

Imagine that you're in court, and without your knowing a bit about it, the judge has been sending secret letters to your opponent: "Pick me as your judge and I'll make sure you save money."

Do you see a problem here?

The National Arbitration Forum and the arbitrators at other arbitration companies depend on the goodwill of Bank Big One. As with First USA, they get not one, not two, but twenty thousand cases just from a single customer, whom they have to please.

And of course no one can go to court. This may be the end of class actions. Typically, the consumer has to sign a clause saying: (1) I waive my right to sue for breach of this agreement, (2) I waive my right to a jury, and (3) I waive my right to file a class action.

"How can they waive the right to a jury?" asks my friend Alan.

They can. The courts uphold these clauses. Indeed, it's impossible to regulate them at the state level. Years ago, long before anyone thought of credit cards or the National Arbitration Forum, Congress passed the Federal Arbitration Act. At the time, it must have seemed harmless. Unions and management liked arbitration—why not promote it generally? Of course, the Congress back then never imagined this. But because the so-called FAA exists, the federal courts have decided that it "preempts" state law. That is, the existence of this well-meaning federal law stops any state legislature in 2006 from trying to blow the whistle on these sham arbitrations.

Isn't "sham" a bit strong?

But these *are* shams. First, in most of these cases there is no "dispute" to arbitrate. Let's say you're behind on your Visa payments. You can't pay. That's not a dispute—you just don't have the money. But under the credit card agreement, Bank Big One decides to "arbitrate."

So there's an arbitration. But these aren't done in a day, like the old arbitrations. These are over in a few minutes. Sometimes it's done by phone. Sometimes they don't tell you at all.

They don't even phone you.

Second, it's a sham because the old arbitration was an alternative to court. And that's why courts uphold this new, one-sided arbitration. Judges use the old rote phrases: "Oh, yes, it holds down litigation." "It's better to avoid court."

But the purpose of these arbitrations is not to avoid court but to facilitate a suit in court. Thanks to arbitration, the banks and companies can flood the courts with suits that they could probably never bring otherwise. Thanks to arbitration, we will all end up in court.

Now, I know this sounds counterintuitive. But remember, the purpose of these arbitrations is to set up collection actions. In the *Washington Post* story I cited above, of the 19,705 claims decided by National Arbitration Forum, the bank had initiated all but 5. I bet that's because most people don't know there is an arbitration clause. No one's going to get on a plane and fly to Minneapolis to bring an arbitration case.

So why's the bank doing it?

Simple: it solves the problem of collecting from debtors in a global economy. Let me explain by telling the story of Ms. H.

A credit card company just filed a collection case against her.

But it's not a suit for failure to pay her debt. Instead, it's a suit to enforce an arbitration award.

What's the difference? It's huge.

But let me tell you about her. She's seventy-two, a schoolteacher, tiny, but with a long face, the kind that would have a chilling effect on children. She brought in her husband too. "He's mentally ill," she said. He beamed over at me.

In 2002, she and her husband bought into a time-share out in Las Vegas. She had to borrow $2,000 from the bank, which loaned it to her at credit company rates. Then her husband became sicker. She had huge expenses. She has paid back over $1,000 on the $2,000 loan. So all she owes now is—

$4,666.00.

That's the balance due.

Now the credit card company is suing her. But it's to enforce the arbitration award. I looked at the award, which is attached to the complaint. It's a smudged photocopy. It says she lost. The bank won. That's virtually all it says.

My friend Alan sent over the case. "You're interested in the National Arbitration Forum. Here's a case."

Ms. H, the schoolteacher, has no knowledge of an arbitration. "I never heard of it," she says. I looked over at her husband, who had a stack of books on yoga and Hinduism and began to mumble about the Four Blessings.

Could an arbitrator have phoned the house and gotten him? "Please stand by. . . . An arbitration is about to begin." But he's incapable of telling us.

He did tell me about the Four Blessings. "The first blessing," he said, "is that we have a body . . ."

And what are the others? But he had already forgotten them. He seems quite happy, but I felt very sorry for his wife.

Meanwhile, the award—attached to the complaint—is as

inscrutable as her husband is. Did this arbitration happen or not?

As I flipped through the complaint, I realized why the bank has to use this roundabout way to sue Ms. H. The bank is in California. If the bank had had to sue her in the old-fashioned way in Illinois, it would have had to attach the original contract. (It could be lost.) Worse, it would have had to attach a bookkeeper's affidavit that the money is due. I could go into court and move to strike the affidavit. "It's hearsay." Then the bank would have to fly out the bookkeeper from California and put her on the stand to testify in person. It's true, in most collection cases, the pro se defendant may not have the wit to ask to see the contract, or to move to strike the affidavit as hearsay. But it could happen. She might get a lawyer.

She might get Alan. She might get me.

In the old days, it would have been a local bank and they could have brought over the bookkeeper. But since we live in a global economy, banks can't keep up this kind of thing, not as the whole country falls deeper into debt and we're all in debtors' court.

If they had to litigate the way they did in the old days, they couldn't sue, or it wouldn't be worth the time, flying out the bookkeeper, and so forth.

But with an arbitration award it's different. The court enforces the award. Now the award is worth something. The bank can garnish wages, or attach the house, or in some other way squeeze an old lady like Ms. H until she pays up. If there's a suit just to enforce the award, Ms. H has no defense. She can't say, "Where's the contract?" She can't move to strike the affidavit as hearsay.

So thanks to out-of-court arbitration, more people end up in court than ever before. Oh, sure, arbitration cuts down litigation. We can't sue for fraud. We can't hit back at payday lenders. Last year in the Supreme Court there was a challenge to an arbitration clause in a payday loan case. The plaintiff said the loan violated Florida law. By an eight-to-one vote, the Supreme Court held that the plaintiff had no right to litigate the fairness of the loan. Why?

There was an arbitration clause. And guess which way the arbitrator ruled.

As in the Florida case that went before the Court, the consumer is out of luck, but the payday lender can bring a suit—that is, a suit to enforce the arbitration award that the consumer now owes $5,000 or $10,000 or $15,000 on what started as a $200 loan.

Yes, it cuts down litigation, and in that sense it's a disgrace.

Of course, in a country that just stripped detainees of any right to habeas corpus, why should consumers have a kind of "habeas corpus" to go to a judge and get them out of the payday loans in which they are imprisoned? It's even more of a disgrace that eight Justices ruled in favor of the payday loan store.

Only one Justice, Clarence Thomas, had the decency to rule for the consumer.

But while arbitration clauses can cut down on litigation, the *real* purpose is to increase litigation. Now that we have arbitration to cut down on litigation, the banks and global companies have all of us in court. Every day, over in Daley Center, on the eleventh floor, the collection lawyers are lining up to enforce these awards. Go over. Sit there. There's no lawyer for the defendants. No one objects.

CHAPTER 9

How We Went to Court as Creditors and Ended Up as Debtors

How did so many ordinary Americans like Ms. H end up in debt? The odd thing is, they started out as creditors.

I have a friend, T, who's a judge in collection court. His friends ask: "What's he doing there?" He's bright, liberal—he could be teaching in a law school. "Yes," he says, "but I want to feel I'm doing something in the world." Every day he sits on the bench and goes through a morning's call: a thousand cases, fifteen hundred. Credit card companies, hospitals, banks—they sell their collection cases in bulk to assignees. They come into his court every morning here to track down people, put a levy on their bank accounts, and garnish their wages. What's he doing here?

He can enforce the rules. He can stop them from attaching a spouse's retirement. Many of these laws come from the old progressive New Deal era. We wouldn't even enact them now.

I used to think that with the collapse of unions, the best thing a young lawyer could do is work for Legal Aid, representing the poor. But lately I've begun to think that if I had it to do over, I'd try to be a judge and ask to go into collections court. Here is where a judge might do the most good.

After all, that's where I'd find many of the union members I used to represent in the plant closings of the 1980s. For many of them, the first time they were ever in court came in these big corporate bankruptcies as the mills were shutting down. In a sense, as litigants, many working Americans started out as creditors.

It's odd to put it that way. But even today, when airlines and auto companies are in bankruptcy, the employees come into court as creditors. With downsizing and "restructuring," I am sure that millions of Americans have had their first taste of court suing their bankrupt former employers.

Think of what companies like United Airlines, Delphi Motors, Republic Steel, and a host of debtors owed to these workers: rights to pensions, rights to health care, rights to severance pay, rights to training and education. In a whoosh, in a single lawsuit, all of these rights were gone, at least for many workers. These Americans, these creditors, all had contracts. But the courts rejected the contracts: literally rejected or invalidated them as too "onerous" or "burdensome."

Sometimes the companies were not even broke. They might be subsidiaries. The parent companies were rich. Many "bankrupt" companies now flourish. The owners walked away from the burdensome contracts and pushed their workers aside.

It was far worse than corporate America going bust. It didn't go bust. Instead, the creditor employee gave up their contract rights. Now, contract rights are property rights, even if they're intangible. I hope they realize, at the University of Chicago, in the Economics Department, that when people lose their property rights, the Rule of Law has ceased to exist for them.

But where is the historian to calculate this shock? At the risk of overstatement, let me make a comparison. In *Postwar* (2005), a history of Europe by Tony Judt, he argues that for a long time after 1945 it was hard for Europeans to recover a belief in the Rule of Law. Under Nazi occupation, property rights didn't count. Savings could be confiscated. Now, I would not dream of equating postwar Europe and the United States in the 1980s, but people did lose some very valuable rights in bankruptcy court. They had worked hard for these "lifetime" rights. It really was a shock when court after court rejected the contracts. Too burdensome. Too onerous. Too "unfair" to the banks, the lenders, the other secured creditors.

Maybe it began to curdle the national character. When people lose their savings, they may start to live for the moment: spend it now. For at about this time, more Americans began to run up debts. Why save? Why work to build up those "lifetime" rights? We could lose them overnight. It's not that workers lost all their earned pensions: the large portion, thank God, was federally insured. But they still lost a great deal, like pay rates, job security, and supplemental unemployment benefits. And they lost certain other lifetime rights, especially health insurance. They had worked a lifetime to get these rights. Now they would have a lifetime to wonder: "How could they take it away?"

Bankruptcy courts didn't always reject the contract. Sometimes, as unions weakened, the employer exercised a unilateral "right" to end the health insurance. It was a right no one ever dreamed the employer would invoke. Yes, I have heard the answers they give in depositions, in several suits our firm brought to get back some of these benefits, whether from the directors or the parent company or some other deep pocket. In my dreams, I can play back the Q and A's of people, sometimes my own clients, who still don't grasp how they lost what seemed to be legal rights. Here's one I can do from memory.

> CORPORATE LAWYER: Mr. P, you say, about your health insurance, it was a "lifetime" right, is that correct?
>
> MR. P: Yes.
>
> CL: You said earlier, you always thought you'd have it?
>
> MR. P: Yes.
>
> CL: I'm handing you Exhibit P-34, which we previously marked, and asking if you can point to anything that says the retiree health insurance is meant to be a "lifetime" right.
>
> MR. P: You want me to look through this whole thing here?
>
> CL: Well, will you turn to page, page . . . let me see, if I can . . . here, I marked it, page 27? *(He pages through a minute.)*
>
> MR. P: Yeah, okay, I'm there now.
>
> CL: If you go down twenty-five lines from the first full paragraph . . . Do you see where it says "Coverage ends if " and then it gives four reasons, and the last one is "the plan is terminated"?
>
> MR. P: You mean, do I see those words?
>
> CL: Yes, did you see them, did you read them?
>
> MR. P: Uh, I see them.
>
> CL: What do you think that means?
>
> MR. P: What?
>
> CL: Do you want to take a minute to read it?

I'll stop it here. Why didn't I object? I can't. I have to let it go on. But my point is that Mr. P and others found out that these rights were illusory. Either the bankruptcy court could reject them or the company could pull the plug.

And just at this moment when these lifetime rights had vanished, they began handing out Visa cards on a bigger scale than before. In effect, working people lost their savings, but thanks to the courts, they now found it much easier to get credit cards instead.

Yes, while the judiciary took away these earned contract rights, they made it easier for the big national banks to give us credit cards instead. The other day a friend of mine was saying to me about the importance of the Supreme Court's 2006 decision in the Guantánamo case, *Hamid v. Rumsfeld:* "It's probably the most important Supreme Court decision of our lifetime." He may be right, but it's not my choice. For me, it's a case of which few people have even heard: *Marquette Nat. Bank v. First of Omaha Corp.* (1978)

Yes, in terms of changing our lives, it may be the biggest case of our lifetimes.

"Oh," say my friends. Sure, *Marquette Bank.* Of course.

What?

In *Marquette Bank,* the Supreme Court smashed, in effect, the interest rate cap on every credit card in the United States. The holding sounds narrow. The Court held that the state of Nebraska could not impose its usury law or its interest rate ceiling on any credit card issued by an out-of-state bank to any resident within Nebraska. (I should say, to be accurate, it has to be an out-of-state nationally chartered bank.) Technically, even after *Marquette Bank,* the state usury laws were "on the books." But if the laws didn't apply to national banks, like First USA, they might as well not exist.

By the way, it was an opinion of Justice Brennan. Yes, it was a great liberal justice who wrote the decision that delivered us into debt. Oh, technically, he may have had a point. In 1978, the Court held that the National Banking Act of 1864—signed by President James Buchanan—"preempts" all state regulation of the credit cards of national banks. Of course, I doubt that on the eve of the Civil War, they were thinking a whole lot about Visa and MasterCard. But over a century later, when it seemed every other bank was a national bank, the effect was to gut every state law on usury. After *Marquette Bank*, even a state bank still subject to state law could whine: "Come on, you aren't going to apply an interest cap to us! It doesn't apply to First USA, or Chase, or any of our competitors!" They could set up out of state. So *Marquette Bank* was like a Big Bang. Now I risk overstating it: by 1978, states were loosening up interest caps. But I doubt the credit card explosion could have happened, or that people could have gone into debt as they have, if even a few brave states could have imposed some kind of caps on First USA, Chase, and their ilk.

Oh, Justice Brennan! How could he do this? In his defense, I should say this: It was 1978. Jimmy Carter, a small-town rural man, was president. He was like our George Bailey, the Jimmy Stewart character in Capra's *It's a Wonderful Life*. Brennan must have thought: Carter will put in a cap. The Democrats in Congress will put in a cap. The Democrats won't let the interest rate go up to 20 percent, 30 percent, 40 percent, or, now for some payday loans, 2,000 percent. Will they? But they didn't get around to it. Already deregulation was in the air. And Carter could not get any of his big bills through Congress at the time. Then the Reagan era began.

By then it was too late.

That's how we lost the law on usury. The usury law is the ur-law of human civilization. From the code of Hammurabi straight up through the Great Society, there has been some legal regulation of interest rates. Now? Nothing. No law. And all of it happened just as people were losing their union-scale jobs. They gave up their union cards and got credit cards instead. With no cap on interest, it is perfectly sensible to hand out credit cards to everyone. In the time of George Bailey, banks did not hand out credit cards or make loans like this, because in the Hollywood movies of the 1930s and 1940s, a banker could only get *4* or *5 percent.* That's all. So it was a big deal for the bank to be paid back. "What kind of person are you?" "What's your moral character?" "Are you reckless with your money?" George Bailey had to vouch for you. You had to meet the standards of Jimmy Stewart.

But now?

Now they'd be glad to give credit cards to the Three Stooges. "Are you reckless with your money?" Glad to hear it! Thanks to a long deregulatory effort that culminates in a final blow like *Marquette Bank,* you'll pay interest not at 5 but at 25 percent, or 35 percent, or maybe higher. If you borrow $1,000 on your credit card, you'll soon owe $6,000 or $7,000 to The Bank. Even if some people file for bankruptcy, the banks can still harvest trillions of dollars.

Besides, they can go to court.

As people stumbled out of corporate bankruptcies as creditors, with their lifetime rights gone, they took the credit cards and began to spend. But this is too simple a diorama; let me argue that there was a tipping point. It is hard enough for Americans to save for the future. In a certain way, the unions had done it for them. Now the unions were gone, and the whole message of the unions—save, put it away for your retirement—had been discredited. Besides, there would be no retirement. Rightly or wrongly, that is the message that many got from the wave of corporate bankruptcies that rejected their lifetime contracts.

Anyway, the real law of the land became collection law. That's why the number of contract cases, which is the category for these collection cases, has now gone up even relative to tort. The states, even Congress, have responded. They love to pass fair debt-collection laws. In a backhanded sort of way, the fact that there are so many laws is a measure of what is going on.

But the fair debt-collection laws do nothing about the unfairness of the debt.

I'm afraid in our firm we have one ne'er-do-well as a client, an appalling person who takes no thought of the future and is always deep in debt. The other day he was sued in small claims collection court. My associate, C, went over to defend him. She's a young lawyer, and it was her first time over there.

"How'd we do over in collection court?" I asked.

"I'm glad I went," she said. "You know, it's like the cases are all defaults."

"Right, they just go in there and default them."

"If a lawyer stood up, it seemed . . . the judge would get upset."

That day, C was the only lawyer who stood up.

"Who was the judge?" I asked.

"A woman—she was young. She had an Irish last name. If people stood up when their cases were called, she'd be annoyed if it wasn't a default.

"Yes," I said. "But she's got a thousand cases on her call."

"Yes, but if someone went up there pro se, she'd start shouting at them. 'Well?' she'd say. 'Do you owe it?' Like that: *Do you owe it?* If it'd been me, I'd have said . . ."

And C took on a judge's voice:

" 'Do you understand why you're here?' "

I thought how precinct captains tell me people don't show up to vote because they don't even know how to use the voting equipment. It's too daunting. You can imagine how it feels to go over to collection court and stand there, pro se, and have a young woman who's not even Irish but took a fake Irish last name so she could be elected, sit there and look down at them and start shouting: *"Do you owe it?"*

Beaten down, people say yes. But do they owe it? Our client, Tiffany M, who had two in-hospital births, was sued each time, for an amount three times what a mother who was insured would have had to pay. Did she owe it? Ms. H who paid $1,000 on her $2,000 loan and now has a balance of $4,666—does she "owe" it?

Tiffany, who was a dropout and an unwed mother, would say: "Yes, I owe it." She is happy, upbeat, and ambitious. She is now an office manager. She agreed to a payment plan that, with two kids, she had no chance of meeting. "Yes, I owe it," she would say. But she had no idea she was paying at least three times what Blue Cross patients were paying.

I'm glad to say that we did quite well for our own client—a feckless friend, not like Tiffany or Ms. H. At first the judge was annoyed that C stood up for him. But then C said, "Your Honor, they didn't attach the contract to the complaint."

That's the rule; the contract has to be attached to the complaint. But since there are thousands of these complaints, it's too much bother to do it. I doubt that a single contract was attached to a single complaint that had been filed with this court. And yet, according to C, the judge pretended to be shocked.

"What?"

Now she turned to the collection lawyer. "Where's the complaint?"

He might well have said, "Come off it, Judge." But he just mumbled, "We'll have to find it."

"Fine," she said, "I'm going to give you a lot of time to find it. I'm putting off the trial here for three months."

This was a victory for us, because now they have to go find the complaint. Yet thousands of others are in here with no lawyers, with no one to speak to them when they shuffle up and hear a woman in black say: "Well, do you owe it?"

One wants to see Jimmy Stewart going up to them and saying, "No, you don't owe that. Come to my bank, and we'll loan you money at just 8 percent." But I'm afraid Jimmy Stewart might just as well never have been born.

My co-counsel C would say, "Do you understand why you're here?" But if it were me, I would want to say, "Do you understand that under the laws of the United States up to the 1970s, this would have been regarded as an outrageous charge? Do you understand this contract with your credit card company, in virtually every other time and place in human history, would have been regarded as unenforceable?"

It galls me that even when I tell my friends about the arbitrators who rule for their client, First USA, over 99 percent of the time, some will say, "But they owe it, don't they?"

No, they don't owe it. One day instead of defaulting they will all show up in collection court and say, "No, we don't owe it." When I left law school, a little book had just come out: *The Death of Contract,* by Grant Gilmore. A young man who knew I was working on this book wrote: "When you say we have moved from contract to tort, isn't that what Gilmore said?" Having forgotten Gilmore's book, I got it via Amazon. Yes, it is what Gilmore said. But he meant it in quite a different way than I did when I was discussing employment law earlier. When Gilmore said that contract was dead, he meant that it was being replaced by a noncontractual notion of "fairness." Bad contracts would not be enforced. But good contracts would be implied even if there were no formalities of "offer and acceptance" or "consideration," or even a complete writing. *The Death of Contract* is Gilmore's wry or detached take on the liberal utopia to come.

But the utopia turned out to be a dark one: not Gilmore's, but a different one, more like Orwell's. Poor Mr. P can't enforce his contract for benefits, no matter how fair and just it is. But poor Ms. H is stuck in hers, in a way that would have been unthinkable to Gilmore and might have caused him to fall out of his chair at Yale when he heard of it. If a contract is to the benefit of the meek and the poor in spirit, it's unenforceable. Mr. P has lost his contract rights, forever. But if Ms. H signs a contract that commits her to pay 35 percent, or 2,000 percent, that contract is enforceable. In fact, as the U.S. Supreme Court ruled last year in *Buckeye Check Cashing Inc. v. Cardegna* involving the payday loan in Florida, it's enforceable by arbitration even if the contract is in violation of Florida law.

In short, when Gilmore said we were moving from contract to tort, he meant we were moving to what lawyers call "quasi contract," or the contract claim as a tort-type claim for fair treatment. When I say we are moving from contract to tort, I mean people are looking for ways to hit back in tort as the old "good" contracts tear apart like tissue while the new "loan" contracts clamp on like a ball and chain.

It's occurred to me to make the rest of the book a kind of handbook of legal ways to "get back." But there are new ones, unknown to me, being developed by other smarter lawyers all the time. I doubt I could give a proper account of all of them. Let me just mention two such ways for working people who have lost their rights to get a little "payback."

Disability: Social Security

Let's go back to Mr. P. Companies used to have such a thing as early retirement: when guys got hurt or used up, they could apply for early retirement and get off their feet. But Mr. P lost his health insurance and his early-retirement pension. So now he can sue for DI, or Social Security disability insurance. As unions collapse, it's astonishing how many people, men in particular, sue for disability. Yes, I say "sue" instead of "apply," because now it's like a lawsuit. In the old days when people applied for disability, they started by looking for a doctor. "You took an exam," an old labor reporter told me. "The doctor filled out a form. That's how you got it."

Now people start out looking for a lawyer. With no early retirement and no full pension based on thirty years and out, the only way "out" for people now is to fight to get on Social Security disability.

One way to measure the litigation is to look at the increase in the number of Administrative Law Judges, who hear these cases. Earlier I argued that the old administrative law was dead and that there were fewer ALJs. The old New Deal part of government, that of the so-called alphabet agencies, has shrunk. Except for Social Security. At the end of the Reagan era, we were down to 750 ALJs. Slightly more than half of the 750 were doing Social Security disability hearings. Now there are 1,300 ALJs and nearly 1,100 are doing Social Security hearings.

Why the increase?

Disability is the new welfare, a kind of AFDC for older men. We got young single mothers off welfare, and we have older men on instead. It may be tempting to think: "It's like the old days when people went out in the street and hoped to be hit by a car." But it's not fake; these people really are disabled. I met an ALJ who told me, "There's no one thing that drives up disability. It really varies state by state. In Michigan, we see a lot of auto workers, factory workers who apply. Why? The companies have them working overtime, longer and longer hours. They're tired, and when you're tired you get hurt. But in Louisiana, it seems like it's obesity. Diabetes."

Down there, it's working poverty: the lowest low-wage jobs, Wal-Mart or worse. People bloat up. They have trouble walking.

And they aren't faking. People really are sick. It's the stress of not having a pension or a retirement. To keep taking on stress is an unconscious way of trying to put yourself out of business. It's a call for help. Or maybe it's despair.

At any rate, when they have gotten themselves sick or hurt or obese enough, they have a chance to "sue" for Social Security disability. It's like a tort suit against the government for not having a social democracy here—a personal injury action against the whole country, for "damages" in a certain sense, for the way we have deregulated everything.

Out of corporate bankruptcies came disability suits.

By the way, the ALJs have formed a union. "Yes, we may be judges, but we'd better organize." Everyone tries to pressure the ALJs to reject the applications and cut down the beneficiaries. It's odd that the Rule of Law may survive in our country only if the judges can form unions.

Front Pay

In much the same way, people who bring employment suits no longer want reinstatement, as in the old days of labor arbitrations. What they want, more and more, is to get "front pay" instead.

What is front pay?

Well, it's the opposite of back pay. It is the pay that a defendant corporation gives an employee for never coming back. After all, in many cases, plaintiffs brought suit because the company just dumped them—they were old, used up. In the old days they would have taken an early-retirement pension and gone away. Now? There's nothing, so they might as well sue.

But these are really suits for pensions, in a way, because the suits seek not so much reinstatement but the new remedy of front pay. The men and women in their fifties who sue know they're unemployable. They're fat. Their feet hurt. They tell the same stories. Sometimes they start to smell.

But in order to get it, people have to go through the humiliation of discovery, of depositions. A Mr. or Ms. P has to show: "I was doing a good job. You treated me unjustly." At the same time, in a subtle way without wrecking the case, Mr. or Ms. P has to get across: "Look, you don't really want me back, do you? Look at me, I'm a mess."

In other words, "I was doing a great job, but please, don't take me back!"

More and more I am bringing what are pension suits in disguise.

If I make a big point about the shedding of pension and health benefits, it is only because this did more than any wage cut to increase income inequality in the United States. The rejection of these contracts and the deregulation of credit made us a nation of debtors. And sooner or later debtors end up in court. "Yes," some say, "but globalization made it necessary." Or global competition made it necessary. Thanks to all the things I deplore, the United States can now compete.

Globalization is the reason that, in court calls all over the nation, judges are shouting at the few who refuse to default: "Well, do you owe it?" But Sweden, Norway, and Denmark are all globally competitive, and people in those countries aren't defaulting in the courts. Even if we are competitive, I doubt it is the only way. Indeed, to the extent that the bankruptcies destabilized people's sense that they had property rights, it seems that our approach should have made us less competitive. That is, we were competitive despite what we did to people's legal rights.

"But we lowered labor costs," you may say. Did we? Think of how the "labor costs" for CEO salaries have ballooned. From a well-publicized recent study of fifteen hundred companies by Lucian Bebchuk of Harvard Law School and Yaniv Grinstein of Cornell, it seems that just the salaries and pensions of the top five corporate officers typically account for 10 percent of that company's earnings. That "10 percent of earnings" just to pay off five company employees is an add-on labor cost that makes our products less competitive abroad. And the sharp rise in this labor cost results from a legal change, or really a change in the law of trusts: the collapse of corporate fiduciary law, which at one time used to restrain the CEOs from raising such costs without any legal limit.

In some rival countries—in Germany, for instance—this fiduciary law that we used to have is still in place. Maybe that's why Germany is better able to compete abroad.

And did deregulation of interest make us competitive? With no more rules against usury, profits in banking and finance soared. It changed the composition of the economy. After all, the banks now get 17 percent, 25 percent, 400 percent for loans, if they own payday stores as many do. Overall, the return to capital became better in the financial sector relative to the industrial. The result is that we put a bit less capital in GM, a bit more in Chase.

And on the subject of capital, even if we did become more

competitive (at least in the financial sector), was it really worth the cost in social capital?

People now feel the ground rocking and rolling underneath their feet. It's not a good thing for the U.S. economy when people experience everything around them as arbitrary and unstable. The more we deregulate, the less stability and civic trust we have. I'm a little suspicious of this notion of civic trust, but there seems to be less and less of it. More and more, it seems, we don't trust government, we don't trust business, we don't even trust each other.

And call it a lawyer's instinct: when people don't trust each other, it ruins them for juries.

CHAPTER 10

Do You Really Want
to See a Jury?

Should we still have faith in juries? As a labor lawyer, I do. It's part of my job to believe in them. "I believe, Lord. Help my unbelief." But except for a few runaway oddities, our juries seem limp. If even an economist like my college roommate can say our juries are behaving "reasonably," it probably means our juries have lost their nerve. At one time, they were set up for the very purpose of redistributing income. Now, it seems, they're scared. Perhaps as the rich get richer, the meek get meeker. Instead of farmers or skilled mechanics or industrial workers in unions, more people work in "services." They "serve." Just as waiters depend on the rich for tips, more of us also earn our livings by currying favor with people higher up. In colleges, we learn to be flexible, to be likeable, to get along. Richard Sennett argues that there is a change in people's character. Of course, there are juries that are exceptions. With 300 million Americans, how could there not be at least 40 or 50 million exceptions? But if Sennett is even partly right, it would follow that juries are less likely to redistribute wealth, at least in the aggregate. Even so, as the stakes get higher, people on the right become hysterical about the slightest risk.

Juries become less and less likely to redistribute, even as the fear of such redistribution grows. Indeed, as juries lose their nerve and hold down verdicts, they lower the cost of not complying with the law. As a result, in this informal way we deregulate even more. The rich get even richer. The unfairness becomes even more extreme. That in turn makes the oddball or exception jury more notorious and subject to presidential attack.

I might as well admit that, like many on the left in Europe, I do not care for juries very much. I'm just terrified to give my real opinion to other liberals—unless, of course, they're lawyers like me. As I write this, I just had lunch with my good friend L. Though a great lawyer, he'd just lost a jury case, in federal court. His client had sued the state which had wrongfully imprisoned him for sixteen years. The jury, mostly white women, didn't give the poor wretch a dime. Nothing. You're wrongfully set up and convicted and in prison for sixteen years? Too bad.

Hey, life's unfair. White people in big houses in the suburbs have their problems too.

While on a court call I saw one of these juries come in the other day. "The typical Northern District of Illinois jury," said my colleague J. "Look at them." All but one were white, suburban, well-off. The twelfth looked Asian in some vague way. I looked over at the plaintiff, who was an older man, an African American, in a suit: middle-class professional, or so I guessed. "He doesn't have a chance," I thought. He knew it too, or seemed to, from the way he looked down. It was some kind of civil case. He lost.

Still, as a labor lawyer I believe in juries. And I tell myself if they redistribute less, it is because they get less of a chance to redistribute. In the pension and health cases I bring, there is no

right to a trial by jury. Perhaps they'll sympathize too much
with the poor old-timers. I'd like to think the jurors would lift
us on their shoulders and march around the room. That's why
in these big benefit cases the corporate world has made sure we
have no jury rights. At any rate, in the pension and health
cases, the jury would have a real chance to redistribute income
in this country but they never get a shot at it.

Now I know I should be pious and inform nonlawyers that
pension cases are "in equity," and in equity by tradition there is
no jury right. But the truth is, they could just as easily be called
contract cases, and then there would be a jury right. The real
reason here is that when it comes to pension benefits, a jury
could simply do too much redistributing.

Meanwhile, in individual discharge cases, or the rag-tag
labor and civil rights law that is left to juries, the jury often is
on the other side. Let's put aside race cases. For these cases,
even I have stopped praying, "Lord, help my unbelief." Let's
take individual employment even for white people. I believe
the studies cited by Lewis Maltby, a friend who heads up a tiny
but terrific little think tank, the National Workrights Institute.
One study he cites—by the American Arbitration Association—found that employees who arbitrated their claims with
AAA type arbitrators won 63 percent of the time, while employees who went to court won only 14.9 percent of their cases.
Now, the AAA arbitrators are the "good old" arbitrators, or
their descendants. Professionally, they are many notches above
the hacks who work for the arbitration companies. Still, even
these people are not as fair as the old union arbitrators of the
New Deal era. Remember, these are *nonunion* arbitrations
which are cited in the study. Yet even they beat filing a jury
case. But here's the bigger shock to me from Maltby's research:
even when a federal agency like the EEOC goes to court, it

wins less often than plaintiffs do in arbitration. Now I admit, when we lose in court, it's not always the jury's fault. The judge may throw out the case.

Why do people go to court instead of to arbitration? For one thing, you can't recover your legal fees if you win in arbitration. For a nonunion middle-class client, winning on arbitration can be a financial disaster. The paradox is that the only people who can really arbitrate are CEO-types who are independently wealthy. Besides, the rich employees have education, look nice, and are more likely to win than ordinary working people. Still, though I know all this, Maltby's finding is quite depressing when I think how hard and unforgiving these nonunion arbitrators usually are.

Yes, hard and unforgiving. But are they more unforgiving than the many juries made up of the kind of crabby old people you used to see in *New Yorker* cartoons?

Here's what I find hard to forgive: the number of people whom our juries have put to death. In some ways I find it harder to forgive than the number of people whom our juries have merely "wrongfully convicted." It's not just that we have so many more people in prison for ludicrously inappropriate offenses—being poor, desperate, a bit mentally ill, and entangled in the drug trade. It's not just that the juries are mean; they are also not using a standard of "reasonable doubt." Look at how many people are being exonerated by DNA tests. How could the juries really have been applying a reasonable doubt standard? I have a prosecutor friend who defends them as follows:

"You're being unfair. I think people on juries try to do their best. But there are two problems. First, the state just has more money. And second, of course, these people really are guilty, usually."

I think I would paraphrase his two points as follows:

First, it's shock and awe. The state in 2006 has a lot more money than in 1906, so these criminal cases aren't a fair match for ordinary people anymore. Besides, softened up as they are by mass media, people are cynical, but also more susceptible to the side that runs the biggest and best commercials.

Second, even many college-educated people can't follow the jury instructions.

For the last thirty or so years, in one academic study after another, it's been clear that many, if not most, jurors find it hard to understand even the most basic instructions. I mean, this not in a law school sense, but in a sixth-grade reading-comprehension sense. It's not legal illiteracy. It's just plain illiteracy.

Or maybe it's an attention deficit disorder. It is certainly very high even as the education levels of jurors are increasing. To me, these studies are the dark secret of the republic. So it's right that they are reported in the most obscure, lowest circulation law reviews, like the one on my desk—*Psychology, Public Policy, and Law,* December 1997: "What Social Science Teaches Us About the Jury Instruction Process." The article, a rare one, is a survey of articles from journals of even lower circulation, and you have to page through to the middle to get to the shocking parts. But it's there. There is 50 percent comprehension, maybe, often much less. And it's not hard stuff. In one study, they go over "reasonable doubt" with the jurors, explain it, explain how it's not just any doubt but has to be a reasonable, serious doubt. Then they test: 75 percent still think it's all right to convict even if they have a reasonable doubt; only 25 percent demur. "No, if I have a serious, reasonable doubt as to guilt, I should not vote that Mr. McGillicuddy be executed." One in four agrees, but that's only after coaching.

While I have picked out criminal law, it is just as true in civil law, where the jury instructions are actually complicated, even to lawyers. So, to many people in prison as well as to civil plaintiffs who keep losing, I can only say this: whether you did or did not deserve what happened, the jury literally (as in the sense of literacy) did not understand what it was doing.

There are no studies, but it's been an ever-growing piece of folk wisdom in the city of Chicago that plaintiffs should avoid juries. For example, in Cook County, there is now "mandatory arbitration" in the mother of all torts, the classic fender-bender case; but either side can file an appeal from the arbitrator and get a jury.

You'd think that plaintiff lawyers would hate the arbitrator. In fact, some of these arbitrators have second jobs where they work as defense counsel for the big insurance firms, like Allstate. Yet according to my lawyer (yes, I'm a defendant in a fender-bender case, but it was a car I lent a friend), it is the insurance company that usually appeals. It's Allstate or State Farm that appeals because Allstate or State Farm can do better with a jury!

Okay, that's all about fender-benders. Who cares? Besides, I'm the defendant. But what about the medical error rate? More and more studies claim that medical error, the really dumb screwup, is a big national problem. If verdicts were bigger, it would bring down the error rate—or at least hospitals would stop cutting the nurse-patient ratio.

But hospitals keep cutting as long as juries don't scare them.

Long ago, an old plaintiff lawyer who did employment cases said to me, "For those company lawyers, getting to the jury stage is the hard part. But for us, it's the reward." Now it's the insurance industry that says, "Oh, the jury—that's our reward."

Well, I no longer think the jury's my reward. It's one reason hospitals seem more, not less, dangerous. Without getting into all the research, it's at least arguable that we're going in the opposite direction of Florence Nightingale's reform. As the jury "deregulates" by holding down the cost of negligence, there may be slightly fewer cases in court, but the cases are more serious.

Of course, it's in employment law that I have a special grudge against juries. As unions disappear, juries have been more and more tolerant of abuses. Perhaps that's the problem. Perhaps it's hard to win these cases if a juror feels that he or she has been violated too. A woman lawyer who brings sexual harassment cases once said to me, "I get up, I tell my client's story, and I know every woman on the jury is thinking, 'She thinks that's sexual harassment in the workplace? Hey, I can top that.' "

But that's the verdict of despair. We're all in this hell together. We can't act collectively to change anything.

Back in law school, I used to read opinions by Justice Hugo Black, the great New Dealer of the Warren Court. In cases like *Dairy Queen* or *Beacon Theatres*, he had this fanatic ideological commitment to put the jury in charge of everything, to run the country through the jury. He thought the jury would tame business. He thought the jury would put the fear of God into a Goldman Sachs. He seemed to imagine that there would be huge antitrust suits, in which juries would take apart these big businesses. I was so excited when I read them: yes, the jury was such a cause. Now I wonder, what was he thinking?! Juries are such wimps. Instead of farmers with pitchforks, we now fill them up with waiters. "Hi, I'm Bob. I'm your waiter for the evening." These people don't want to bash the rich. They want to be nice. They want to please. And the last thing on earth they want to do is what Hugo Black expected: to check and balance the establishment, to kick it in the pants. But he came out of the 1930s, and jurors now are not farmers with pitchforks, but waiters with pitchers, people who are serving or in services, corporate team players and the like.

In a way it's amazing that juries aren't even worse.

Consider that, unlike the old days, we now have jurors who don't vote. They've not even registered to vote. They've never read a paper. They've never even read a whole speech, printed out in the paper, as speeches used to be printed out in their entirety in Lincoln's or Black's time. Indeed, they've never heard a whole speech, as distinct from a twenty-second sound bite. In schools, even in colleges, they never had a class in which they had to follow, or even hear, a legal or extended argument such as a jury might hear in court. But that's not what disturbs me.

What disturbs me is they don't even have opinions.

A while ago a friend of mine who teaches debate in college said, "The biggest problem I have in teaching debate is that the kids don't have any opinions."

"What do you mean?"

"When they come to college, they've never read a paper. They're like their parents. They're going off to the business world. They take classes in business, and what they begin to pick up, over time, is that to fit in, they shouldn't have opinions."

If they have opinions, then they won't fit in. And they'll have to struggle even harder to pay off their student debt.

Some kids do have opinions, of course, but as to the rest, it's his biggest problem as a teacher. So what's his method? "We don't begin debating. I assign them a paper, like the hostage crisis in Iran under Carter. They go off, research, and then they have to stand up and give us a report. I try to get the student to think, 'Say, on this one little thing about Iran, I'm an expert. I . . . I can have an opinion about this.' "

"So," I said, "once they get an opinion on one thing, they can get an opinion on something else as well."

"Exactly," he said.

But if he's right, it must mean that on juries we have people who simply have no opinions, never had opinions, in order to be nice and go along. That may be why a few alpha-type friends who get on juries in Manhattan have said to me, "Oh, you're so wrong about juries! I was just on one, and these ordinary people were so wonderful!"

Translation: "Well, I got my way and the others went along. They were so nice about it too!"

Maybe I'm being unfair. People work longer hours. They don't have the time or leisure to participate in civic life. I'm a labor lawyer. I sympathize. Still, it's fair to say that our juries are now full of people who have never cast a vote. I found this out in a curious way. For years I thought that only a registered voter could ever get jury duty. That's why at family parties there's a loudmouth second cousin who loves to say, "Hell no, I'm not registered to vote. I don't want to end up serving on some jury."

And so it used to be. But as the number of trials went up and the number of registered voters went down, something had to give. At some point in the big lockup of prisoners, we began to run out of jurors. At least we didn't have enough registered voters to keep putting people into jail. I learned all of this, because for years, I had wanted to bring a suit to do this very thing—require nonvoters to serve on juries too. I wanted to shut up the people at the family parties. But when I began to be serious about this case, I found that nonvoters were already on juries. A jury commissioner at the time told me, "Look, we still use registered voters, but we have to supplement the lists." So in Illinois, a typical state, every year the state sends the jury commissioner a list of everyone in the county with any kind of state photo ID. Then the commissioner does a mailing or a canvass, basically to find out: "Are you a U.S. citizen?"

So nonvoters were already on juries. Now I was alarmed: is that what I had really wanted? It's weird to have nonvoters on juries. For many people the first civic act in their entire lives will be to send someone to the electric chair.

But still, I can hardly give up on juries. For one thing, if the United States does not have a true democracy, it would be dangerous to give up on juries. As I keep arguing to no avail, we do not have a true one person, one vote type of Constitution. We do not have a republic or a democracy in the sense other countries do. If we did—if we had majority rule and real social democracy—we could and would dispense with juries. That is, if the democracy is strong enough, there is no need to call up juries to act as a check and balance or a counterweight to the state. That's the argument for the jury. Until the United States is a functioning republic or a true social democracy, it is too risky to give up even the light check that the jury system imposes on the state.

But I wish we could.

I now feel silly that I was so swept away as a law student by the opinions of Justice Black and others who argued for the jury. I can see how it may seem to work if there are other "countervailing powers," to use the old phrase: the old unions and granges and city political machines from which American jurors used to come. It may have made even more sense in the time of Tocqueville's America, when people in small towns served on local juries, not just once but ten or fifteen times. It really was an office, and for people who read and listened to political argument, it was fun. But now in the jury waiting room, no one is even picking up a paper, people are listening to their iPods, and there are four or five television sets turned on, to different channels. No wonder people can't follow even basic jury instructions, which were developed for a different type of human being, a linear thinker of a hundred or two hundred years ago.

Yes, it's making everything worse. But there is the occasional wonderful jury that keeps . . . oh, I don't know, it bears witness to something in the human spirit, I guess. "Is there anything we can do to make it better?" Though I hate to waste time fixing the jury system rather than the Constitution generally, I suppose there is one simple thing we could do.

Spend money.

First, in most states and in the federal system, the greatest scandal of the legal system is the jury pay. In Illinois state courts, the pay is $17 a day. "That doesn't even cover parking," my sometime co-counsel Scott says. But even if there were free parking, the pay comes out to $85 a week. That means, in a sinister way, we are able to weed out the poor from jury duty. Even over in the federal court, the pay of $44 a day is outrageous. Working people in this country live from paycheck to paycheck. For at least a quarter of the country—maybe even a third—service on a jury is a paycheck disaster. Of course they try to get out of it, literally to pay for groceries. And employers don't pay them.

It's fine for the left to push for more liberals on the bench, but how about working people on juries? That might help the cause of redistribution. Every juror should be paid tax-free the median take-home pay of a worker in this country: $651 a week.

Also, if they were paid, they might then be tranquil, or composed enough, to follow what people are saying in the trial. To pull in a temp from a secretarial service—a mom with two kids—and put her on a jury at $17 a day is almost to guarantee she's going to give the whole case only a part of her attention. It is the equivalent of sending a child off to school with no breakfast. No wonder the kid is spacing out in class.

For judges, the jurors will be easier to handle. People are less cranky when they are being fed. And plaintiffs may find that people are more generous when they are being fed. A jury, like an army, marches on its stomach. That's why the corporations want the pay to be low.

But won't many jurors get the $651 a week on top of their own weekly pay as well? Fine. So be it. Let jury service be a windfall for working people. Let them *make* money. If you pay what is in effect a bonus for many, it means that they will take it even more seriously. For the first time in decades, the United States will be sending a signal to those who end up on its juries: "This is how important we think it is."

But we should do more than spend money on the supply side; we should spend money on the demand side too. In particular, the right to a jury should be free to any party. It should be free not only in the big important cases but in little ones like small claims. Right now, the fee for a jury is going up, $300 or more for small claims. Make it free. Yes, even if it costs more money. If we spend serious money on juries, we will start to change the outcome of cases as well—that is, we will bring more lower-income people onto juries and make them take their duties more seriously as well.

Being a Democrat, I have to be in favor of juries—but only if we start to pay them like kings.

No, I'm not a secret defender of juries—since, if we get rid of them, we're left with nothing but judges.

CHAPTER 11

But Would You Rather Get a Judge?

It's tiresome to be cynical about judges. Besides, some lawyers are past the point of merely being cynical. After all, is it so new to be cynical about judges? The old New Dealers were, too. For a long time, the legal realists used to argue: "Oh, judges! They just act in their own economic or political self-interest." Or: "They don't apply the law." That view was in vogue in the 1940s for a while. Yet now the situation is arguably worse.

If I were just cynical about judges, I might still trust them, at least to act in their self-interest. At least our legal system would be predictable. I could function as a professional. I could tell my clients, with a certain confidence, "This is how they'll rule."

What's frightening nowadays is—I don't know. For one thing, I'm not as cynical as the old New Deal realists were; I think judges really do act sometimes on the basis of ideals. The bigger problem is that, ideologically, the judges we have today are all over the lot. This is partly because the political system has become so polarized and gridlocked. So the cases I file get randomly assigned to "centrist" judges and "radical right" ones in no foreseeable way.

Long ago, in a famous book, *The Common Law* (1893), Oliver Wendell Holmes Jr., a legal realist and a cynic, wrote: "Law is nothing more than predicting what judges do." But here's my problem as a lawyer: How can I predict what judge I'm going to get? As I will try to explain, it's a bigger problem in federal than in state court. When I file in a Chicago federal district court, I could get a Carter, a Reagan, a Bush I, a Clinton, or a Bush II appointee.

Let's say there are twenty-one judges. With seven of them, I could win. With seven, I could lose. With another seven, I could toss a coin. Am I going to be in the court of a judge whose hero is William Brennan . . . or Clarence Thomas? In a sense I don't know what legal system I'll end up in.

Never has the Rule of Law been such a lottery. Nor is it as simple as Republican versus Democrat. Sometimes, to make it even more of a crap shoot, Bush or Reagan might pick a moderate. For me as a lawyer, never has it been so hard to predict to a client what the law will be.

At the same time, it's less important which judge I get, because so much of the case now takes place out of court, in pretrial discovery or oral depositions. The real trial now takes place in the private offices of big law firms.

There's no judge around. There's no one to keep order. I can't even get the opposing lawyer to sit down. The other day a lawyer came over and stood right over the witness. What do I do? Tell him to sit down, or ask the client to stand? And there is not much limit to what the other side can ask. "We want to see your e-mails." "We want you to go into your hard drive." If you threw out a letter or deleted an e-mail two years ago, you start to think you may go to jail.

The very conduct of a case is like a tort. In depositions, I see my clients insulted, beaten, and left half dead, and all I can do is pour ointment on their wounds. Sometimes I can go to the judge and say, "Your Honor, they're brutalizing my client!" But I don't dare go too often. I might start to irk the judge, who, after all, has three hundred cases and is not particularly interested in my tales of torture.

This unregulated pretrial torment is in fact the true trial. The true point of discovery is to discover how well the client can survive. People ask, "When do we go to court?" It's hard to say to them, "You will never go to court."

It's hard to exaggerate how deregulated and privatized our U.S. litigation has become. In other countries, the judges take the initiative. They say, "Here is what I want to know." In Germany or France, it's the judge who runs the case. The lawyers are there to answer questions. In Germany, for example, it is an ethical violation if a lawyer even speaks to a witness (any witness) outside the presence of a judge.

Compare that to the United States, where a witness can be hauled in by a lawyer, questioned, threatened, and more or less violated, with no judge around at all. Which legal system is more likely to pump up people's rage?

Yes, there are exceptions. In the United States there are a few judges who instinctively act as judges do in Europe. "This is my case. Here's what I want to know. I'm running it. Here's what I think the issue is. I want a ten-page brief by Monday."

"Your Honor, it's Friday, I was going to . . ."

"*Monday.* Is that clear, Counsel?"

When I get a taste of my own "European" medicine, I resent these judges, but at least the cases move along. Yet even these judges can't do much about the out-of-court interrogations.

And while in the United States there are rules for discovery, the rules mainly say: there are no rules. Anything goes. And the more the cases are deregulated in this way, the more money counts. So, paradoxically, less court means more court. There is now a limit of seven hours for the deposition of a given client, but the cases can go on, outside of court, in law firm offices, for years.

Imagine Justice in an empty courtroom. She is wearing a blindfold, and no one is around because the real trial is going on in another part of town. Today our judges all wear blindfolds. Few know or want to know what is going on.

Still, before filing a case, I'm afraid of what kind of judge I'm going to get—Reagan, Bush I, Clinton, etc.—even though I know he or she won't stop the beatings. In that way, I suppose it's like the Bible. This allows me to sit here and write philosophically about the declining importance of the judge. I can go to a yoga class and try to breathe slowly: Calm down. Relax. Since I'll never even see this judge, it doesn't matter who I draw.

But of course the judge does matter, even if there is no trial. In the federal courts now, there will be about 100,000 civil cases filed. Only 2,000, or 2 percent, will ever go to a trial, a bench trial. Though I cannot get numbers, I bet half of these trials are not even before judges, but before assistant judges or magistrates. In the federal courts, the judges are too busy to try cases. What are they busy doing?

They don't run discovery.

They don't hear oral argument.

They don't even try cases.

So what do they do? They write. They're all writers. Scribble, scribble, scribble. And they write opinions tossing out the cases. Or they don't toss out the cases.

And I emphasize the word "opinions." They are *opinions*.

Yes, formal, impersonal, even scholarly—but they're not to-
tally unlike the opinions of William Safire or Maureen Dowd.

And based on these opinions, we win or lose. Also, they can
sanction me. Even if no one ever sees a judge in our system, a
single bad draw can wreck my whole practice, if not my life. So
on a day-to-day basis, in my office life, when I'm not sitting in
a yoga class, the unpredictability of who I'll draw is terrifying.
In that respect, if I had practiced law at any other time in our
country's history, I would have suffered less from this terrifying, random unpredictability of the kind of justice I get in any
given draw.

How did this happen? Simple: For the last forty years there
has been no majority party in this country. Unlike Holmes's
day, which was the McKinley era, or the liberal age that began
with FDR, we have had an unbroken period of divided government. There has not been the like of it since before the Civil
War (maybe not even then). In 1968, Kevin Phillips wrote
The Emerging Republican Majority, always hailed as prescient
but not really prescient enough. Phillips was wrong: no Republican majority or any other majority really emerged. No one
party has ruled, or has been able to rule, for long.

So no one party can pick a bench. Since no one party can
pick a bench, there is no coherent legal culture. Bush I picks his
140 or so. Clinton picks his 140 or so. And Bush II picks his.
Isn't that good? We get variety. Perhaps if the two parties were
closer together, it might be all right, but they're too far apart.
So far apart now we have to use different words to talk to these
judges. And the outcomes are really far apart. It comes not
just from the law that they apply but from the facts they regard as important.

What Thomas Kuhn argues in *The Structure of Scientific
Revolutions* applies to judges as much as scientists. Kuhn says

that scientists do not truly observe or record the facts in an impersonal way. They have paradigms, or theories as to how the world works, and these paradigms tell them which facts are important and which are not.

In the same way, I would say, an older Reagan judge is looking for certain facts that a Clinton or even a Bush II judge is not. A libertarian free-market judge is looking for facts that a moral-values judge is not. It's not so much that I have to argue different law but different facts as I run from case to case trying to keep all the dishes spinning.

Until I actually know the judge, how can I tell the clients if they even have a case?

What has made a single legal culture so impossible is the same thing that has made one-party rule impossible: too many people have dropped out of civic life. And because we don't have enough voters, the GOP can be competitive with relatively fewer but more committed voters, while the Democrats end up appealing to everyone else, with no message coherent enough to hold together a majority. Over time this means that we usually get divided government—deadlock, with no single party being the majority. And if no single party can be the majority, no single party can pick the bench. As a result, no single legal culture can emerge.

And that's what makes it so much harder to practice law.

At any rate, we ended up with two legal benches. Or two cultures, each out to undo the other's Rule of Law. And it's even more complicated than that. I'd like to say that, thanks to the appointments of Carter (left), then Reagan and Bush I (right), then Clinton (left again), and then Bush II (right again), we have judges who are left and right. If only it were true! But there is no left-wing bench. Like Carter, Clinton did not appoint lawyers on the left—like his old friend, Peter Edelman, or his classmate, Lani Guinier. He did not, or could not, because the Senate would have blocked him. Clinton did not have the political capital to spend.

Yes, he and Carter put a few liberals in the lower courts, but not in the Court of Appeals or even in the Supreme Court. Take Justice Stephen Breyer, a Clinton appointee. Breyer was a big champion of deregulation, the bane of this book. He is a Democrat who went along with dissolving the state. Now, Breyer is a decent man. He's certainly against torture. But when Clinton named him, my law clerk friends told me that conservative scholars in Law and Economics rejoiced. To them, Breyer was not just the best possible Clinton appointment, but the best possible appointment!

That's why there is no real "left" up on the Court.

So when I say there are two benches or two cultures up there, I mean moderate right (David Souter) versus extreme right (Antonin Scalia). Or the American Bar Association versus the Federalist Society, the right-wing legal group founded in 1982. Up there the "left" is the ABA, which in any other time in our history would be the bastion of the right, as it was in the days of William Howard Taft. The new right, the Federalist Society, is far to the right of this old right. My allies, the people on my side, are the lawyers at Paul Weiss making $800 an hour and defending CEOs who make at least $50 million a year.

What kind of left legal culture is that? It's better than no left—at least we're all against human torture. At the appellate level or above, it's not so much left versus right, as a split on the right. This is often the case in history. Think of England in the 1930s, with Churchill backed by Labour going after the old Tory right. Or think of the Gaullists and the French left at war with Pétain, the premier of Vichy France. I realize it's a bit extreme to invoke those dreadful times. My point is this: the real battle at the moment is between the right and the right.

For me as a lawyer, the problem is that if the "bad right," or New Right, wins, it will not stabilize the legal culture. It will not lead to predictability, which is the very thing I want as a lawyer. Let's put aside the right of contract; contract rights, at least of working people, mean nothing to the New Right. And let's put aside trust law, which they despise.

Believe me, they could unravel these legal doctrines even more, and they probably will. But that's not what worries me. The danger with this right is that they are very postmodern, and, being postmodern, they don't know what they want.

I could say, for example, that they think government is illegitimate. But it's really worse than that. In a sense they think *everything* is illegitimate. Or at least they think it's all subjective. This is especially true in the Federalist Society, among the "kids." (I mean people twenty-five to thirty-five or so.) When people like me talk about the good and true, they stick out their tongues at us. Others just cover their ears.

"That's just your opinion! We don't want to hear you moralizing!"

Like Moses in the Old Testament, they want to pick up the Ten Commandments—that is, the truths of liberalism—and smash them on the rocks. "Stop moralizing!"

If we cite the Fourteenth Amendment, they just sniff: "And who wrote that—Lincoln?" That's a cue to laugh.

If we bring up the Declaration of Independence, they say: "Oh, these truths are self-evident? Well they aren't evident to us."

If we dare bring up the Geneva Conventions, they say: "Are we going to let these little countries tell us what to do?"

Nothing is sacred, least of all the sacred texts, the "American scriptures." They only like the parts that lead to some absurd or anachronistic result. They work on little law review articles to "prove" the Fugitive Slave Act is still in effect.

Perhaps the world seems as arbitrary to these kids on the right as it does to some of my old blue-collar clients. I think of these old steelworkers who go down to the riverboat casinos. I bet they drive by the University of Chicago just as the kids in the Federalist Society are holding one of their meetings. They could tell the kids: "You bet the world is arbitrary."

And perhaps the kids sense it just as well. It's not that they really believe the Fugitive Slave Act, for example, still ought to be in effect. But wouldn't it be delightful to argue the case?

That's the big difference between the old ABA conservative right and the New Right. In the old ABA right, we liberals actually do think *some* truths are self-evident.

It is true about some truths. Don't ask us which ones, though.

And for just thinking so, we wonder if we're out of it. We clap politely when someone mentions *Brown v. Board of Education* (1954). We know we're against torture and we're for *Brown*. "That's self-evident, right?" But the kids don't clap. They don't think anything is self-evident. They love to blaspheme. And they laugh when Thomas or Scalia uses the constitutional-law equivalent of potty language in front of us adults.

A small example: the dissent by Clarence Thomas in *U.S. Term Limits, Inc. v. Thornton* (1995). It's when I read this dissent that I saw how big the gap was between the Federalist types and us. In *Thornton* the issue was, can a state legislature impose term limits on U.S. congressmen who happen to be in the congressional districts of that state? A few years ago, the answer to this one would be easy.

No! A mere state legislature can't pull a congressman out of Congress.

Yet if that's what *Thornton* decided too, it was a very close call, by a vote of five to four. Four justices signed a Clarence Thomas dissent claiming that Arkansas or any other state can pull a U.S. senator or House member out of Congress. It's not just the main argument that woke me up. It was the kookiness of Thomas's little footnotes and asides. For example, his riff on "We the People"? It doesn't mean "We the People of the United States." Is that what you thought? The Founders really meant, We the People of *Virginia* and We the People of *New York* and so on, and not We the People of the United States. Thomas even wonders if it is grammatically correct to use the term "United States" as a singular noun. Maybe it's plural. Maybe we shouldn't say, "The United States is Number One!" Maybe we should say, "The United States *are* Number One!" As well as Number Two, Number Three, and so on, down to Number Fifty. And the bigger point to which all of this leads Thomas and the other Justices: It is not "We the People" who are sovereign. How can sovereignty be in the people of the United States? Forget what Lincoln said at Gettysburg, that we have a government of the people, by the people, for the people. It's not true!

Then what's left? We the People of Arkansas and the other forty-nine. We the Peoples are the fifty sovereign powers. If that sounds like an argument for secession, it should. Thomas's dissent more or less quotes here from the work of John C. Calhoun. Yes, the Darth Vader of American history! The Senate champion of slavery, the rival of Henry Clay and Daniel Webster. It is the great slave master himself whom Clarence Thomas quotes.

Calhoun—who was the most violent of all in defending human bondage!

Not that I would have caught it. My old college professor pointed it out. "He's quoting Calhoun."

"You mean an African American Justice is quoting Calhoun?" I said.

"It's a little odd," he said. But he shrugged as if it were the way of the world.

Yes, and it's a little odd that the sainted Sandra Day O'Connor signed on to it. It's easy to imagine the law clerks giggling as they write. It was Calhoun who said, "Not everyone is entitled to liberty." Maybe Thomas or one of his clerks will quote that line too on the day that Justice Roberts and the Supreme Court decide that the Thirteenth Amendment is unconstitutional. Yes, think about it: did a *true* majority in South Carolina agree to free the slaves?

In the Federalist Society, some of the kids even call themselves "neo-Calhounians." This gives me the creeps. Didn't Calhoun himself look a little like Lucifer? In my grade school history book, I remember seeing a picture of him, old and sick, being carried into the Senate on a cot. "Oh, my goodness, it's the devil!" Calhoun's the one to whom Andrew Jackson so famously raised his glass and said, "Liberty and Union, now and forever, one and inseparable!"

Or maybe that's what Daniel Webster said.

Anyway, Calhoun was scary. Now, he's like a rock star to these kids.

The difference is this: Calhoun was serious about slavery and states' rights, whereas the kids are just ironic. Indeed, the New Right is not sure if they want states' rights or not. As many point out, the Rehnquist Court began turning against the states in its final days. It's a puzzle. Why would the neo-Calhounians turn on the states?

Well, part of the reason is—the states were doing drugs.

Look at Oregon and California. Some states were heading toward same-sex marriage. The Bay state was the gay state. If the Federalists began turning against the states, it's because the states stood in the way of the culture wars they want to bring.

Or at least they did until the 2006 election.

Meanwhile, in law and economics, and in the chamber of commerce, they really turned on the states. Until state class actions could be stopped, no businessman was safe. So the irony is that the New Right was moving toward a New Deal version of national power. But this was a New Deal black hole. That is, when the federal government deregulates, it means the states must deregulate too. That's what the New Right means by the doctrine of federal preemption. If we in Washington, D.C., don't do it, you in the state capitals can't do it, either.

Now, it may be that after 2006 with a Democratic Congress, the right will go back to the good old Rehnquist days of fighting for states' rights. But I doubt it. They may realize, or should realize, that they are stronger at the national level than they will ever be at the state level. They will never have California, and they may not hold on to Florida. At the state level, they will never control enough states even to rule over a majority of the population. But at the national level, they have a chance. This is because the Constitution "overrepresents" the parts of the country where the New Right is strong. It overrepresents the New Right in the Senate, even without the filibuster, but especially with it. It's not at the state level but at the national level that the New Right is strong, and if it stays disciplined, it can often be a majority, because its ability to block things can make the Democrats, the party of government, look so ineffectual. The Constitution works in such a way that the Republicans tend to look like leaders, in command, and the Democrats tend to look like fools, who can't do anything.

But the very fanatic and disciplined quality that helps the New Right succeed at the national level backfires in the states. Unlike the national government, the states do operate by majority rule. Outside the South, where the New Right is in an actual majority, it is harder for the New Right to take power just by operating as a disciplined minority that over and over makes the majority party look ridiculous. What the New Right can do in D.C., it can't do at the state level.

They might have pulled it off: taken control at both the national and state level. But in 1962, the Supreme Court decided the cases that led to reapportionment in the states. The states, but not the national government, have to abide by one person, one vote. The result is that at the state level, but not at the national level, there is a chance for effective majority rule. The New Right does not do very well under these conditions. Even if they take power, as they sometimes do in Illinois, they do so as moderate Republicans, virtually a different kind of political party than the one that competes for power nationally.

Over time, as the effect of one person, one vote has taken hold, the blue states have gotten bluer. Perhaps it's because the nation is less white. But also thanks to reapportionment, the states are modern, up-to-date, in a way the federal government is not. Like European countries, many states now have new or relatively new constitutions. If the U.S. Constitution did not have such a depressing effect on democratic life, we might appreciate how much better the states are. Slowly, the right's love affair with the states has begun to cool off. It may have lasted longer than made sense, politically.

I make a lot of all this because so many of the judges on the New Right and others in the Federalist Society no longer know what they want to do. They're in even more confusion intellectually than we on the left are. At the very end of his life, William Rehnquist himself began to back away from states' rights. In some of his last opinions, he wrote that a federal law like the Family and Medical Leave Act did apply to the states and their employees. This was a complete reversal of what was to be the legacy of his court. Why did he switch, even rule against himself in a way? "Oh, family leave was different," a law professor said at a talk I heard. "He has a daughter who's a single parent. He ended up taking care of the little boy, while she went off to work. He really found out what it was like to be a single mom."

It must have happened on Christmas Day too.

But I doubt that's the reason Rehnquist flipped. I think that Rehnquist, sick at heart, had come to see that he and the New Right had to turn their fire on the states. In the end, they realized that the very nature of states' rights had changed. Instead of being the right to own a slave, it was now more likely to be the right to get stoned. Why would the New Right want to defend the right to get stoned?

So the older Federalists like Rehnquist have had to murder their darlings. In their case, there's a kind of tragic dimension to it. I can almost feel sorry for Rehnquist, who seriously believed in what he did. But I don't feel sorry for the younger Federalists. Whether it is states' rights or any other doctrine, I don't think they really care.

That's why they scare me. Unlike Rehnquist and the older Federalists, it seems they don't believe in anything. There is nothing to moor or stabilize them except to shock us, the liberals. They will even defend torture if they think it will nettle us. I like to think the younger ones started out wanting to do good, or at least to do public policy. Rather than go into the private market, they preferred the academy or government. Even on the Supreme Court, the New Right Justices, with the arguable exception of Roberts, shrank from the private sector. It's odd how Scalia, Thomas, Alito, and so many of the younger Federalists seem to have such a distaste for life in the business world. They deregulate, but I doubt they have much idea what all this deregulation is for.

The genius of the founders—or I should say, the funders—of the Federalist Society was to figure out how important it was to get a kid a job. Like Scalia or Thomas or Alito, the young kids on the New Right don't want to go into business; they want to do public policy. They want to do what liberals do. So along comes Mr. Federalist to say, "Oh? You want to do public policy? I've got a nice foundation job for you." The next thing the kids know, they're at the Cato Institute. In a certain way, the New Right is like the Old Left, but it's undergone a sex change.

There is another way these kids are like liberals: in a sense, we passed on our values—our relativism, our scepticism, the way we scoff at a certain type of moralizing. The Federalist kids take our own values and use them against us. "You taught us everything was relative," they say. "Well, we apply the point to you. You want 'equal' protection. But why protect anyone? You're against torture. But isn't it all relative? You say 'We the People.' Who are 'We the People'?"

That's why I'm fascinated by the culture wars in the academy. The lineup there is the opposite of what I see in court. In the universities, liberals scoff at moral absolutes. But in the courts, we argue for absolutes—we argue for human rights, yes, and even natural rights. We defend the prisoners. They defend the guards.

We have to be pious Anglicans. They get to be Zarathustra. To some these culture wars might seem a bit precious. Well, they *are* precious. Yet I think they can also poison the way people behave. It's one thing to attack Reason; it's quite another to stop being reasonable. Also it's hard to be postmodern and have a stable Rule of Law. If everything is so relative, a liberal construct, then contract law, trust law, all of it can go. It justifies deregulation. "But wait," someone will say, "isn't it true you people on the left have been postmodern and relativists just as you now say these kids on the right are?" It's true, but when we on the left do it, at least in the history of this country, it's been harmless. Or, it hasn't caused any harm to the poor in spirit, the meek, those in prison, and the like. But when the right is postmodern and starts to scoff at fixed values, not only is our Rule of Law less stable, but the little people get hurt.

Now, this relativism about everything can be up-front and over-the-top, as with a Scalia or a Bork. But to me it's just as bad when it's polite and button-downed. I am thinking of the new appointees, Roberts and Alito.

Let's start with the over-the-top ones, Bork and Scalia. Well, let's skip over Scalia, who's lately become too over-the-top, as he goes around on lecture tours and gives us the finger. Besides, he seems happy now. So let's go right to Bork, a sadder, more wounded character. It was Bork who let loose on human rights law in a memorable speech, at the American Enterprise Institute in 2001. The whole idea of human rights, he argued on that occasion, was repellent. When people talk about it, he feels "nauseous." Or since I don't want to overstate, he feels "somewhat nauseous."

Why would any human right, such as the right not to be tortured, give anyone indigestion? It was his way of giving us the finger. It was telling the young in the audience, in code:

"Don't these liberals with their talk of human rights make you want to puke?"

We make them want to puke for the same reason that Jefferson in the Declaration of Independence (a document that many of them hate) makes them want to puke. We like the Enlightenment. We want to think for ourselves. The human race is making progress in figuring out what is right and wrong. Over on the New Right, they hate it when we talk like that. Look at the way they cling to the doctrine of Original Intent. It's not that they really believe in Original Intent. They just don't want the rest of us to use reason. The idea of Original Intent is that we should think about things in the same way the Founders did. We have to discern their intent, however ridiculous it is to figure out what the Founders in 1787 would have thought about global warming now. There is no space here to go into why this gets so preposterous. I could say: "The flaw is to explain the Founders' first-order intent about the Constitution in terms of their second-order intent as to how they wanted to deal with gay rights two hundred years ago. That is, the issue is not what they thought about gay rights in 1787, but whether and to what extent they wanted us to be free to deal with the questions of our day. The original intent was not to have Original Intent. After all, they were men of the Enlightenment. And as Kant explained, the very purpose was to liberate us from perpetual childhood, specifically in trying to discern Original Intent."

But our case against Original Intent—that it leads to a perpetual constitutional childhood and is absurd—is exactly what they want. They, or some of them, want it *because* it is absurd. It is postmodern Original Intent. It's a halfway house to nihilism. It's a delicious thing to use reason as to why we can't use reason.

With Original Intent, they can mock us: "You don't like it? Then change the Constitution." But it's now impossible to change the Constitution—that's the problem. Nor should we blame the Founders. When the Constitution was adopted in 1787, it was amendable enough. Indeed, they very quickly added an entire Bill of Rights. But now we have not thirteen but fifty states; and because of the way the population is distributed among the fifty, a relative handful of people can block any amendment to the Constitution. In theory, twelve states containing a mere 6 percent of the population can block any amendment.

In other words, it takes virtually unanimous consent. And those who argue for Original Intent know this very well. So what? Let the Constitution be our tomb. Anyway, that is the point of Original Intent: we have no right to think. I'm being unfair to some, but not so unfair to others. It's not even our liberal moralizing they want to stop. They want to stop the use of reason, or I should say the use of "public reason," a phrase of the liberal philosopher John Rawls.

Stop moralizing. Stop all this thinking. Stop it, stop it—stop! They don't want to hear us talk.

Of course even in the Federalist Society, they're not all like this. Look at Terry's Law. It's still hard to believe. Congress passed a law to try to get a court to put a feeding tube in a young Florida woman who was in a permanent vegetative state. For some of the New Right, the very absurdity of Terry's Law was its appeal. If Terry's Law was "law," then there is no such thing as law. A friend of mine teaches a course in federal courts at a night law school. "I could teach the whole course out of the Schiavo case," he says. He means that Terry's Law broke every single doctrine about the nature and relationship of federal and state law. Why were so many on the New Right ready to drop Original Intent?

They drop Original Intent if they can find a better way to

show that there is no there there, no set of neutral principles that anchor them to anything. In part that's why Scalia and Thomas vote to strike down more laws than Breyer or Ginsburg, the two Clinton appointees. It's on the New Right where judges are more likely to throw the bombs—even when they don't know where to throw them, or why.

Still, to be fair, even on the New Right, some people balked at Terry's Law. In the Eleventh Circuit, which covers Florida, Bush's own appellate judges helped the Clinton judge below to get rid of the Terry Schiavo case that was filed under the special law. The message seemed to be: "You in Congress can make the laws, but we decide the cases. Stay off our turf." I mean, we can't have a legal system if they keep passing things like Terry's Law.

And here I better say that even in the Federalist Society, there are all types, not just the wild-eyed fanatics, but a few sober ones as well. After all, if we're not on the Supreme Court or in a university, we have to live in the real world. I often draw judges on the right and they're fair enough to me. They have three hundred cases on their calls, and we are all trying to get out of here and go home at night. Besides, we have to have a right—even I know that. We can't all be on the left, and I say thank God for that. It's good to have some balance.

But what troubles me is that the near-nihilism in the law schools can even taint the pragmatists. If Scalia and Bork are the flamboyant version of a New Right, there is a way that the new chief justice, John Roberts, is unmoored too, but in a different way—a much nicer and more button-downed way. Roberts was a corporate lawyer, after all. He may not even like the Federalists. At his confirmation hearing, he tried to come across as one who always followed precedent. For him, the law was a fixed and settled thing. He believed in "minimalism."

Yet, whenever senators asked him to give the law on a point, it seemed he could not commit himself to anything. The more he testified, the more alarming it became. The law kept shrinking into a tinier and tinier thing.

"I can't say, Senator."

"That's unsettled."

By the end I wondered if even breach of contract was unsettled. Maybe there is no such thing. It's not that I think Roberts is a nihilist, but his minimalism is a kissing cousin. Everything is up for grabs. There's no law that's nailed down.

And if nothing is nailed down and the old legal doctrines of contract and trust are under enormous pressure, Roberts is the least likely of all judges to save the precedent he touts. In a different world, a different country, like the America of the 1950s, he would have been a different judge, a certain honorable type of conservative, someone who would try to defend precedent. But so far he seems like a weak judge, with no real commitment to precedent, or anything else—except to lie low and let the others push him along.

Perhaps I'm wrong.

But the more minimalism there is, the less law there is. Or at least the old legal doctrines will keep breaking down. The more the older law breaks down, the more litigation there will be, directly or indirectly. It may take the form of "little" cases, pro se cases, cases in collection court. But it's more litigation all the same. Whether the minimalists like Roberts win out or end up losing to the nihilists and the bomb throwers, the outcome will be the same. There will be less law. There will be more deregulation. Fewer of us may see the judges, but more of us will be in court.

CHAPTER 12

So What Is Our Judicial Philosophy?

What is our judicial philosophy, on the so-called left? Of course we liberals don't really need one at the moment. It's like being in the French Resistance. We can talk about it later. Right now, let's just push out the invaders. Still it's an interesting question: Do we have a philosophy or view as to what judges ought to do?

It's annoying that we have to come up with a judicial philosophy. "Just focus on electing people," you say. But the problem is, we can't. After all, we aren't in a true democracy or a normal kind of republic. In *Bush v. Gore*, the Justices reminded us that we literally do not have a legal right to vote for president. And at the same time that we have no majority rule, we also have a constitution that's a blank. It smiles and keeps its secrets about matters that a modern constitution in any other country would decide. Even a country like Uganda or Gabon. Okay, they may have to worry about issues like female genital mutilation, but women have constitutional equal rights, and even seats reserved for them in the legislature. Our constitution has so little in it, and it can't even be amended to deal with abortion or the environment. We suppliants come and beg it to say something to us about health, or education, or anything that modern people care about at all. Speak! Say something. But that dead white male of a thing, our Constitution, rolls over like a lifeless whale.

On right and left, we have to make the darned thing speak. That's why there's such hysteria as to who gets on the Court.

Now some will gasp: "You don't like the Constitution?" Of course I like the Constitution, probably more than you do. No one else but me would sit home on a Friday night and read the Federalist Papers just for fun.

I worship the Founders, all right?

But we are helpless to amend our most basic legal document to settle what should be our Rule of Law now, so we end up experiencing the Rule of Law as arbitrary. Thanks to the unamendable nature of the Constitution, we're always in court. The fights keep going on, and it drives people nuts. It pumps up the rage. Think of *Roe v. Wade.* It takes up an issue, abortion, that's been settled in every country but here. The right has a point in saying that *Roe* is not legitimate. After all, there's no literal right to an abortion in the Constitution. On the other hand, the left has a point in saying that *Roe* is legitimate. There is no right to privacy in the Constitution, either.

Yet we all "agree" that there is a right to privacy. When Bork said there was no such right to privacy, the U.S. Senate shot down his nomination to the Court.

So now even Scalia says there is a right to privacy. But even if he does, it's still not in there, literally. We just agree that it is, even if it isn't, because if we didn't, no one would accept the legal system as legitimate. In a sense we all pretend there is a right to privacy.

Let's go on to *Roe.* On the one hand, *Roe* is reassuring; indeed, *Roe* is like a rock. In this age of deregulation, it is the only constitutional law or principle that really has stayed put since I got out of law school. So *Roe* is stabilizing. It's a way of resolving a question that it would be impossible to resolve in a fair way by a constitutional amendment.

But then *Roe* itself is a kind of deregulation. It is a law that says there is no law. So *Roe* is destabilizing. Like any form of deregulation, it leads to more litigation. That tends to happen with any deregulation to which many people feel they did not give their consent or even have a chance at an up or down vote.

Even though I'm on the left, I can understand why people on the right can think the Rule of Law is arbitrary. "Where does this come from?" They rage. They rant. They want to tear down the rest of the legal system. They're so mad, beating their tom-toms over *Roe* and voting on the right, that they fail to see that now they have fallen into debt, that they have to shop at Wal-Mart, that they have no pension.

But they hate *Roe*! They feel that somehow they've been robbed by us. And we on the left have paid a terrible price.

And because they have to experience the Rule of Law as arbitrary, they have made sure that the rest of us experience it as arbitrary too. They have put in the very people who make government weaker. "What you did to us, we will do to you."

The flip side here is just as true. If there were no *Roe*, people on the left would also feel they were robbed. It would be just as destabilizing politically if there were no *Roe v. Wade*. More of us would find out how little control we have under our Constitution.

Let's just take the right to privacy. In a sense, since it is not in the Constitution, the right to privacy, which is the basis for *Roe*, is not legitimate. But that's an extremely dangerous thing to conclude. Let's say the right to privacy is not legitimate, even though all of us on the right and left need the right to privacy almost as much as we need the right to breathe. If the right to privacy is not legitimate, then it may lead many of us to conclude: "Well, maybe the Constitution is not legitimate."

How in 2006 can we be under a Constitution that has no right to privacy? Yet though we all agree there is such a right, we also know that if we tried to push for an amendment with the right to privacy we would never get it through. Indeed, we could never get the First or Fourteenth Amendment through again. We could not get Article I or II or III through, either. It is essentially too hard in a country of 300 million to get what would more or less require a unanimous vote.

Unpleasantness could follow.

That's why I'm writing a chapter about judicial philosophy, or "what should judges do?" We need a judicial philosophy because we have a Constitution that denies majority rule and cannot be amended. It cannot be brought up-to-date. Except in trivial ways, there are only two possible ways to amend the Constitution.

1. Have another Civil War, or War Between the States, and get the Blue states to impose it on the Red states, militarily. Like in 1865.
2. Get unanimous consent from everyone in the United States.

While this would be harder than going to war, it is in effect what is required. The Senate and the House and thirty-eight states would have to ratify. In the end, it comes down to the fact that senators and/or states representing just 9 percent of the population base could block any substantial change in the Constitution. That's why the Equal Rights Amendment died. It's simply impossible to amend the Constitution in any serious way. So we have judges to do it for us—which is another reason why we experience the Rule of Law as arbitrary. But as the centuries slide by, even the judges can only do so much. The Constitution becomes ever more dottily out-of-date. Frustrated, though not knowing why, we work ourselves up into an ever bigger political rage.

Every other constitution in the world is more up-to-date than ours. In Europe after 1945 they all got new republics, with hot-from-the-printer constitutions. In Asia, the newly independent countries got them, too. They have a right to health care. A right to employment. And most of the other rights set out in the United Nations Universal Declaration of Human Rights. Other nations, like Uganda, take up the rights of women and children. Some address the environmental crisis we are all facing.

What does that mean?

First, they have norms, in writing.

Second, they have consent. It was not easy, I'm sure. A constitution takes, and should take, a supermajority. But there is a huge difference between a constitution that takes a supermajority and one that cannot be amended except by a more or less unanimous vote.

None of this would be so bad if our Constitution, like other constitutions, provided for majority rule in the legislative and executive branch. But it doesn't. Historically, the Senate has blocked majority rule. Again, the math of the Senate is against majority rule.

Long ago I worked in the federal bureaucracy. The old-timers would say, "The Senate is where everything goes to die." Forty states representing 9 percent of the population base can block any law. On the left, we miss that fact: the kind of country we want went to the Senate to die. Except for a few years in the 1860s when there were no Southerners in it.

As a result, the majority has never ruled. Not even in the New Deal, which Senator Carter Glass and his fellow Southerners simply shredded. They tore up FDR's original bills, which called for so much more than the New Deal ever got. And that was when people really did vote! Starting several decades ago, the majority gave up trying, and the people who should be the majority started dropping out.

If our young vote at the current rate when they hit middle age in 2026, and if their children vote at a correspondingly lower rate, we will have only a third of the country voting even in presidential elections. Not half—a third. That's why we need the courts.

We need judges to do what the majority would do, if the majority ruled. After the New Deal we began to beg the courts: "Please do what we would do for ourselves if we had no Senate blocking the Southern lynch laws even in the 1950s, if we had no Electoral College, if the Constitution were not so impossible to amend." We had no choice but to do it with race. It was the Senate that kept the race issue on the boil. Yes, I know it's elitist. People blow up: "Let's go to the people, let's have majority rule," and so on. But we can't go to the people because there is no majority rule. The problem is, if we have no majority rule, we have to guess what "we" would do. But this gets even trickier, for if we did have majority rule, it would change us. We'd likely be a different people: more like the Canadians or Australians, or even the Dutch. But since we don't have majority rule, no one really knows.

That's been the puzzle for lawyers on the left. We look for some external, objective standard: "What would a majority do, if we had majority rule?"

Now, there are at least three, or maybe four, answers. Please bear with me as I go through them. Believe me, I would rather tell stories about lawyers making $800 an hour and people getting deposed, but I think a book like this should also discuss justifications for judicial review. Well, then, how could a judge today figure out what We the People would do?

Follow the Crowds

That's a fancy way of saying, "Let's look at what kind of laws other countries have." It is a hot issue. Should the Supreme Court look to foreign law? Let's take an issue like: Should we have capital punishment for children? Scalia and Thomas go into a rage on this point: "We should never look at what other countries do." And in his confirmation hearing, this is one of the few points at which Roberts dropped his boyish charm and began to sneer: "Why should we care what the law in Sweden is?"

Now, I'd be happy to let the Swedes decide this one for us, but Roberts is right: it is irrelevant what the law of Sweden is, just as it is irrelevant what the law of Malaysia or Sri Lanka or New Zealand is. It is illegitimate for a court to say, "They don't kill kids in New Zealand, so let's outlaw it here."

So it's okay if Roberts wants to rant about the law of Sweden: to hell with Sweden.

But if Sweden, Malaysia, Sri Lanka, New Zealand, and every other country has a rule against the killing of kids, then it *is* relevant what the law of Sweden is, not in and of itself, but as part of what one would call the "wisdom of crowds."

Now, I know there is a best-selling book called *The Wisdom of Crowds*. And I admit that I am easily attracted to the kind of glossy idea that gets in a handsome magazine. Anyway, here is the claim: in a group of people, the average of the guesses made about the weight of a prize heifer bull at a state fair will turn out to be the weight of the bull exactly. So a crowd will get it right. This is not so far from the view of Aquinas that the agreement of reasonable people as to what is right or wrong should be the basis of what we call "natural law."

Is it? Of course, Aquinas would not consult just the people at a state fair.

Still, you see the point. If the wisdom of all the crowds in Sweden and every other nation is to oppose the state's killing of kids, maybe this wisdom of the crowds generally should be the wisdom here. Yet in a country that clings to the idea of American exceptionalism, it's hard for us to accept that we should do what other countries do. It may humble us to admit that we may not be so exceptional after all.

But what may be exceptional about us now is that, unlike Sweden and all the rest, we do not allow the wisdom of our own crowd to filter through the Constitution. The Founders did not believe in the wisdom of crowds—no one but Thomas Paine really did at the time. Now we all do, or so we say.

Of course, in this approach we have to exclude countries that do not have "true" majority rule. So that's where it gets tricky. It's easy to drop China. I would also leave out Russia. I'd also keep out many of the "democracies" of Africa.

But to find the true wisdom, I would keep out any country that fails the test for a republic as set out by Abbé Sieyès in *What Is the Third Estate?* This world-famous pamphlet, barely read in our U.S. schools, came out at the start of the French Revolution. In a way, it's a one-up on our Federalist No. 10. Here is the test of the Abbé Sieyès: a country is not a republic unless it has at least *two* institutions based on one person, one vote, and *no* institution that violates the principle of one person, one vote. Under the Abbé Sieyès's test, only the U.S. House of Representatives would even conceivably be one of the two institutions he would demand for a true republic; and even the

House might fail because the gerrymandering is so extreme. So the United States is not a true republic. The UK would also not meet the test: while it has a House of Commons, Sieyès would insist upon two such institutions. Why? With just one, with single-member districts, there are many scenarios in which a minority could rule. Thatcher pushed the UK into more of a U.S. type model, but she did it with only about a third of the popular vote. So the United States and UK do not belong in any test that would tell us what a majority in a true republic would do.

But a startling number of countries with "modern" constitutions are republics under the test set out in *What Is the Third Estate?* Go through Europe. Asia. They have the necessary two institutions, or if there is only one, as in the UK, then it always has a version of proportional representation so that a Thatcher-type minority could never override the real majority.

If someone could collect the rules and norms of the countries that do meet this test, then we'd have a list of what a true majority, in its wisdom, would want. It's a wisdom that our Constitution is set up to skew and distort.

Do the Right Thing

That's another way of saying, "Look to a philosopher." And in my own life in the 1960s a lot of us looked to John Rawls, a Harvard philosopher who in 1971 wrote a very big and important book, *A Theory of Justice.* And it still appeals to me—let's just think it through! The idea here is, let's reason from first principles, or let's say "premises," which everyone has to accept. We don't have to look at what they do in other countries.

When I got out of law school, I bought *A Theory of Justice*, and while I could never get through the whole thing, it was wonderful to own. I had it up on my shelf in my little cubicle of a law office, when I was twenty-six years old. Sometimes it is important just to own a book like this, even if you never read it.

Still I knew the basic argument from law school, and from earlier articles: Rawls asked us to assume we were all in the Original Position. I could imagine him saying: "Shut your eyes." And from the Original Position we would think: "Well, I could be dropped out of the sky into any house, so what kind of income distribution would I want there to be?" The answer is: "I'd want enough inequality so that the market would work, and we'd have colleges and cars, but I wouldn't want so much inequality that I could end up in Calcutta."

The point is: get outside yourself and figure out what kind of safety net there should be. Well, it's a good idea, but I don't think it works as a way of deciding what is "fair," or certainly what the courts should do. There are two problems that I see with Rawls's argument. (I am sure there are others, and I would know them if I were a philosopher, but I'm just speaking as a lawyer.)

First, how do we get people to play this game?

The whole thing about the Original Position makes me think of Wim Wenders's movie *Wings of Desire*, which has angels standing on the clouds over Berlin and looking down below and being so detached from it. And I'm sure if I were up there in the Original Position, I wouldn't care what the distribution of income would be. Not even having a body, I'd have no interest in playing the game.

And of course once I was in the world, and I was a white upper-middle-class American with a law degree, I'd say, "Well, I have no interest in playing the game."

Second, even if we did play the game, what's the answer?

I don't know, in the abstract, what the distribution of income should be. And I'm especially suspicious of turning the decision on this over to an angel or someone even more bodiless, like an economist. I don't know, and they don't know, what will work. Or, if it does work now, will it work tomorrow? There's a problem with all models. In the abstract a certain model works, but it may not work on earth.

Now Rawls wrote before the "Chicago school" of economists began moving into legal studies. The way Rawls set up his argument, he seems to invite these people in: "Bring them on." Well, it worries me to "bring them on." Besides, I don't know the right trade-off in every case between efficiency and equity or fairness. I am not sure there even *is* one, at least in every case. Anyway, it's odd for a humanist to start an argument that, in the end, is never going to end. Is free-market America or social-democratic Europe better? Which part: Arkansas versus Sweden or Rhode Island versus Portugal? It's impossible to argue or reason it out, and at moments our side will seem to lose. That's a danger. Kids may start off reading Rawls and end up raving like Ayn Rand.

That's why I go back to consent, democracy. Not the wisdom of philosophers but the wisdom of crowds—at least in a true republic. But since we fall short of a "true" republic and can't get the right answer that way, it's tempting to turn to Rawls.

Did people really turn to him in the late 1960s and 1970s when he was publishing his articles and then his book? "Come on," some will say, "you didn't quote him in your briefs, I bet." No, of course not, though our teachers did in journals and they still do write about Rawls.

He was big at the time. Why? People were trying to decode what the Fourteenth Amendment was supposed to mean. It was a mystery. What did "equal" in the words "equal protection of the laws" really mean? The Fourteenth Amendment was this strange thing that we had just uncovered and begun to feel and touch, the way explorers might approach the monuments on Easter Island.

What was this thing, the Fourteenth Amendment? It was like the start of a draft for a whole different Constitution. It seemed to invite us to think about equality, or equal protection of the laws, as if we were in the Original Position. And of course to the right, this is the opposite of Original Intent.

They can try to limit the Fourteenth Amendment, but it comes out of a whole different worldview—a radical egalitarian view. Its origin is not just in abolition but in all the U.S. history that went before, like Andrew Jackson's war upon the National Bank. For a century no one would go near these implications.

But in the 1960s, why not?

There is a debate now as to whether the Civil War really resulted in much. Yes, the slaves were freed, but they probably would have become free anyway. And at any rate, apartheid began again. But without getting into this whole argument, I'd say that the Civil War certainly had a huge impact on the 1960s: a hundred years after the Civil War was over, we rediscovered these amendments. We had a legal revolution. It could have gone further, but then we lost our nerve.

Equality was all the rage. Incomes had become more and more equal since the New Deal. Indeed, in terms of redistribution, the New Deal actually came into its own in what we called the post–New Deal. And as equality became the rage, it seemed to some that maybe the Fourteenth Amendment, this strange unfinished "constitution," would let us do much more. That's why the 1960s were so exciting. Yes, of course, the Fourteenth Amendment prohibited discrimination based on race. But didn't it also apply to wealth? It wasn't just Lincoln's amendment, but Jackson's too. And maybe it was ours. Maybe we could argue: "We don't just have a 'negative' right to be free of the state, but a 'positive' right to have the state spend a little money as well."

The law held out a promise of giving us a right to a certain amount of welfare. It's now hard to believe—I hope younger readers will trust me—but even the GOP seemed to go along. Or at least Nixon did. While he was invading Cambodia, he and his adviser, Daniel P. Moynihan, offered up a Family Assistance Program, which was a guaranteed minimum income. Why would Republicans want to redistribute wealth to the poor? I guess you had to be there. I'd just say that at the time, unlike now, equality was all the rage. The income gap was shrinking. Maybe it addled people's heads. It changed the way we talked. And lawyers began to make ever bolder arguments in court.

Lawyers started to argue for equality for its own sake. And the argument almost won in the San Antonio school district case. The poor in Texas attacked the unequal funding of the public schools. In particular they attacked the use of a local property tax that kept poor districts from spending a proper, or "fair," amount for the children. Here is where lawyers tore out arguments from Rawls and others to press for equality, for justice as fairness.

But we lost, five to four, on that saddest of days, when the Court decided *San Antonio Independent School District v. Rodriguez* (1973). Oh, it was a terrible thing, when justice-as-fairness went down in flames. In *Rodriguez*, a bare majority held that the equal protection clause did not require the state of Texas to spend the same amount for education of all. The local property tax was safe. Inequality was still the law.

Yet think how close it was, five to four. With just one vote, our whole history would have changed. Even the fifth vote, the swing vote of Justice Powell, seemed to be a close one. He even noted that the inequality in Texas seemed to be diminishing. He seemed to suggest he might rule otherwise if the inequality became worse.

Of course it did become worse. The Reagan era was bad, and the post-Reagan era has been even worse. In Illinois, the disparity in spending per student widens every year: it now ranges from $4,000 per pupil in the poorest district to $15,000 in the richest. And this gap is sure to grow.

It's too late now to go back to Justice Powell. The idea that the Court was protecting local autonomy is even sillier in this age of state and federal standards and No Child Left Behind. It is quite unfair to set the minimums at the state and federal level but require the funding at the local level.

But there's little hope of changing the thinking in federal courts. No one argues now for equality as such. Few people would even argue for justice as fairness. *Rodriguez* was the end of using the courts to do what a majority of the people in a true republic would do. But there is still another kind of judicial review. It is a humbler thing. It would not end disparity in wealth. It would not impose any substantive result.

It would just more forcefully defend people's right to vote.

Bring Back the Carolene Products Case

In this great old 1938 case, Justice Harlan Stone lays out what the new role of the Court should be. It would be up to the Court from now on to make sure that We the People rule. Yes, it would be the paradox of such judicial review. For it would be up to appointed judges, the elite, to let the majority be the majority. The Court would make sure you and I could participate. That would be the basis of judicial review. The role of the

Court would be "to clear the channels of political change." It was all compressed into small type and dropped into a footnote, the famous "Footnote Four." The idea of Footnote Four is that the Court was now committed to expand the right of all of us to participate.

And indeed, the Court *did* expand the right to participate, from 1938 on. It kept going until it shortchanged the kids in the public schools in *Rodriguez*. After that, the Court stopped expanding the right to participate, even the right to vote.

It's been downhill more or less all the way to *Bush v. Gore*.

A nonlawyer may wonder: Well, what was *United States v. Carolene Products Co.* about? The case itself is of no matter, but it happened to be a chance for one of Stone's clerks, a kid of twenty-four, to help his judge slip in a little footnote. The purpose of the note was to tell people: "From now on, here's what the Supreme Court's going to do."

Remember, for a good fifty years or more, up to 1937, the Supreme Court had done nothing but block majority rule. It is odd how people on the left criticize us lawyers: "Let's stop trying to win our victories in court, instead of using majority rule," and so forth. I have two answers. First, in American history, the left has rarely won in court. The central fact of our legal history has been that, over and over, the left actually gets clobbered in court. Let me wave a limp hand over decades of cases where courts would enjoin labor strikes, throw out minimum wage laws, and even at the end try to outlaw the whole New Deal. Second, if we had true majority rule, we would use it. It's the not having it that sends us into court.

But in 1937, the Supreme Court gave up fighting the imperfect majority rule there was. It decided to make peace with the New Deal. Though FDR had tried to pack the Court, the justices ended up saying, "OK, from now on, we'll leave all your New Deal laws alone."

But if the Court was not going to throw out progressive laws, it was unclear what the Court would have to do. And footnote four was a statement of intent: "From now on, we on the Court will try to promote majority rule."

It's like going from the second to the third play in *The Oresteia* trilogy. In the second play, *The Libation Bearers*, the Furies come raging on stage and run around shrieking and calling out for vengeance. But in the third, *The Eumenides*, they abruptly turn sweet, and bring blessings on the polis, and try to spread all the happiness they can. In Footnote Four the Court said, in effect, "We're sorry for being the Furies and trying to suck the blood out of people. We're going to be the Eumenides from now on."

And here is what Footnote Four promises: "From now on we will intervene to make the democracy more democratic. First, we're going to do the opposite of what we did before. We're going to knock down laws that 'restrict the political processes which bring about change.' Second, at the same time, we'll try to stop the laws that pick on 'discrete and insular minorities.' "
And this time, the Court didn't mean employers. In effect, the Court was saying: "One day we may go after Jim Crow laws, but we don't have quite the nerve to do it now."

Now, my rendering is a bit loose. But the scheme of it all is laid out in a book by the late John H. Ely, *Democracy and Distrust* (1980). And unlike *A Theory of Justice,* this one I've really read, not just once but three or four times. It's the best book I know as to what the Court should do.

So why didn't we keep pushing Footnote Four?

The short answer is, we thought we had exhausted the possibilities. But as I hope to show, that was a big mistake. And because we gave up on Footnote Four too soon, we got our great country into the mess it's in today.

As Ely has pointed out, Footnote Four has two distinct goals:

"majority rule" and "no bashing of minorities." The majority should rule, but racial minorities should vote. But ultimately there is one goal: "more participation." And from 1938 onward, this is what the Court began to push for—not just letting people vote, but letting them march in the South, or just letting loose a flood of talk.

Younger readers may say, "I don't remember reading this."

It's not taught that way in school. But the Court didexpand the right to vote. Indeed, voting was the least of it. As John Dewey says, voting is the least important thing a citizen does.

So Ely would describe even *Brown v. Board of Education*. Jim Crow laws got in the way of "more participation." And in the 1960s, the Court expanded the right to vote. It struck down poll taxes in the South. It opened up party primaries. It eased voter registration a lot. I gasp to read some of the things that the lower courts were doing. A few years ago I had a voting rights case, so I had to go back and read these old voting rights cases from the 1960s. In Mississippi, a federal court held that the election judges had a duty to help the illiterate voters mark their ballots! In Chicago, a court held that Puerto Rican voters now had a right to vote in Spanish. By 1969 the Supreme Court even held that people in the Cook County jail awaiting trial had a right to vote!

Of course, they'd yet to be convicted. But imagine any court, much less the U.S. Supreme Court, caring about this now. Last year the Court would not hear a civil rights case alleging that the state of Florida was keeping 600,000 ex-felons from voting, for the obvious reason that ex-felons are black.

Never mind that such exclusion of these men in Florida was the way Bush was elected president once, and maybe even twice. In 2005, the U.S. Supreme Court would not take up the case.

But in Earl Warren's time, the Court held that voting was a "fundamental right." "Fundamental" is a code word that means if the state touches the right with so much as a feather, the Court will stomp the feather to death with a brick. Fast-forward to the present. In our Seventh Circuit, in a case I lost, the court of appeals scoffed at our argument that the Constitution gives people the right to vote. Indeed, in *Bush v. Gore*, the majority went out of its way to say that Americans really have no "right" to vote for president. The states could choose not to let us vote for president. (Yes, it's in the opinion.)

But back in the 1960s, the Court did a much bigger thing than just expand the right to vote. It also changed the constitutions of the states. In *Reynolds v. Sims*, the Court held that the state legislatures must be elected on the basis of one person, one vote. In one stroke, the United States had a new "constitutional settlement." In a sense, all fifty states had to meet the test of a republic as defined in *What Is the Third Estate?* They all had to have institutions based on one person, one vote.

By the way, if *Reynolds* is right, then, logically, the federal government is, in a sense, "unconstitutional." In fact my old college teacher S used to say: "One day, they'll declare the Senate unconstitutional." It's not one person, one vote. Over the years, as I saw so many good laws get blocked in the Senate, I often thought: "In *Reynolds*, why didn't they go the rest of the way?" At Yale Law School, there was a professor who used to ask on an exam: "List all the ways the U.S. Constitution is 'unconstitutional.'"

But at least the Court had the nerve to declare most of our state governments unconstitutional. Of course, the effect of all this has been ruined by the continued failure to have a true republic in the nation-state that rules over all of us from the top:

it's this nation-state that "overrepresents" the right. It's still true even after the election of 2006.

Anyway, it was an amazing thing for the Court to push this kind of republican rule. Look at all the state constitutions it scrapped. After all these years, our new justice, Samuel Alito, is still mad about how far the Court went. Of course I'm just as mad it did not go all the way.

During the 1960s, the Court kept trying to push up the voting rate, especially in the South. Indeed, the Court did more than we appreciate. With respect to the voting rate, the uptick from the Court helped offset the downward slide that we were getting as unions and granges and big city machines went into decline. Of course, one can argue that the Voting Rights Act of 1965 was more important. But without the courts to push it as hard as they did, the act could have been a dud. And, of course, Martin Luther King Jr. and Bayard Rustin and people marching, all that helped. Fine, let's say King and Rustin and the NAACP and SNCC and the whole civil rights movement was vastly more important than Thurgood Marshall arguing in the courts. But the whole purpose of Footnote Four, or just what Marshall was doing as a lawyer, was to help unleash a movement like King's. That's the point. Besides, even if a case like *Brown v. Board of Education* did not have the impact of the Civil Rights Act, it delegitimated the opposition. It turned the opponents of King more or less into outlaws. It's *Brown* that got the federal marshals in. Gandhi really did have to engage in true civil disobedience, for the British Empire did not send in federal marshals to control its own people in the field, the way the U.S. federal government did at times, at least symbolically. If only because of the symbolism of *Brown* and other cases pushing for participation, King's civil disobedience was arguably less disobedient than Gandhi's.

What's the moral of this story?

First, always read the footnotes, like Footnote Four. Second, the clerk who wrote it was just one year out of law school. It may be the only chance you get by a mere footnote to change the history of the world.

But by the time I was twenty-four or twenty-five, some of us had gotten tired of hearing about Footnote Four. People had the right to vote, didn't they? I took it for granted. Blacks now had civil rights. And as more of us picked up on Rawls, *Carolene Products* seemed more and more . . . well, a bit old-fashioned.

But it was a big mistake to think so. And it led to a mistake in the way the *Rodriguez* case was presented.

It should have been presented as a case about the right to vote. I know that this argument was made, but it was not the principal argument, as I read the case. The principal argument was the negative one, namely, that the state could not discriminate on the basis of wealth. Or it was a positive one, that people had a right to a public good. It was an attempt to put in place a new paradigm. It was an attempt to argue in a thrilling and new way about the distribution of income.

But we could have just argued it as a boring old continuation of Footnote Four. We needed it for majority rule. We have to spend the money more equally so that more of us could be citizens. Like *Brown*, it was not about wealth but about participation. But even to argue over wealth, or to do it as it was done, was bound to scare off the judges. It sure scared off the ones appointed by Nixon, at least.

Maybe there was never a chance to win. Maybe one thing we had failed to realize about Footnote Four was that this footnote was not free. It costs money to have a right to vote. It costs money to have participation. The right to participate in a democracy, at least in our time, necessarily requires a certain amount of money from the state.

It may cost more and more to get a republic that will deliver the wisdom of crowds. We used to teach civics in the schools. Now, in most schools, we don't. John Dewey warned us that the primary purpose of our education system should be to get people to participate. Now, by and large, we don't really try. We assume that in our country people just participate more or less naturally, at no cost. They can do it as easily as breathing.

In fact, it takes a lot of effort to get people to start breathing. It takes more money and effort than we are spending today with No Child Left Behind. We can't count on the unions or the granges or the big city machines anymore to get people to the polls. We can't count on these once-mighty organizations to look out for the majority's interests—to tell them, "We've thought it all out for you and this is how you ought to vote." For the republic to work now, ordinary citizens will have to figure it out themselves. And it's going to be harder for them to do it, because in the middling classes, people are materially better off than in 1938, when Footnote Four appeared. I mean they have more material goods, or at least private ones, more iPods, video games, TV, and other distractions. Civic life now takes more effort. At the same time, people have to take a greater responsibility for their own government. Once, we could let the labor unions, the granges, and other mass-member associations do it for us. But except for the churches, they are generally too weak to help guide us politically.

It's difficult in every country to produce citizens, to have these true republics. But it's much harder in our own. For one thing, because the Constitution frustrates majority rule, we lack so many of the things that give people a stake in participating elsewhere. We have a small public pension: worth about 39 percent of our income on retirement, compared to an average of 70 percent in other countries. The things that bind people to their particular constitutions in other countries, such as free health, free education, the right to organize into unions, are more or less missing here.

So what seems so simple, Footnote Four, letting the majority be the majority, gets harder every year. When I was a kid and was trying to read Rawls, I was thinking that perhaps we could straight-out argue for a European-type democracy. I mean an "FDR type" social democracy in which people would be full social citizens with legal rights to jobs, pensions, health care, and the like. But now I realize it will be hard enough to keep in place a Lincoln type democracy—in which people are simply political citizens, and read the paper and stay informed and even serve effectively on juries and come out to vote.

All of this is to explain why we lawyers on the left should have stayed with Footnote Four. It is the only form of judicial review that we can get away with—or should get away with, I might add. I know that some will say, "We did *Carolene Products*, didn't we? In fact, we pushed it as far as it would go. Blacks have the right to vote."

Of course, one could argue whether blacks really have had the right to vote in the recent elections. But I understand the point. And my answer to it is: "We have to do *Carolene Products* all over, or we have to take it up again." We have to be more imaginative in using the law to get a true majority to participate, to carry on the work of expanding the right to vote, and getting people to care about and feel they want to vote at all.

If we don't, if we can't expand participation, the base on which the legal system rests now will get smaller and smaller.

That means the Rule of Law is more uncertain. The law itself becomes less stable. Yes, it's the argument here that unless we can figure out a way to pull in more people and stabilize our political system, more of us will be in court.

We will go on, unhappily, living in the "Fourth Republic."

CHAPTER 13

Living in the Fourth Republic

I must say it again: being a lawyer, I'm not against litigation. That's just ridiculous. It's like being for or against cholesterol—there is the good kind and the bad kind.

And by the way, I'm not against torts!

What I'm against is the older forms of contract and trust law breaking down, resulting in costlier and meaner kinds of tort. What I'm against are the new and more irrational forms of litigation, which come out of the breakdown of this older law. What I'm against is our excess of deregulation. The deregulation of labor as unions disappear. The deregulation of charity as it is turned into businesses run by MBAs. The accidental deregulation that comes from the fact that the government is weak.

Too many people end up in court when this deregulation occurs and when the government is less able to execute the laws.

Well, that's what we're getting. And because it's so costly and ineffective, this litigation backlash is a kind of national road rage. Usually it doesn't work. There's not even a final judgment, and people end up feeling as hunted as Bill Clinton when he was living on the run and being pursued by Ken Starr.

As the older Rule of Law disappears thanks to deregulation, we end up with litigation as a form of stalking, with people in the process feeling violated as they never did before the modern deposition. Indeed, the techniques for torturing people out of court used to be quite limited.

Why did our legal culture become so much worse? At least one reason—a partial reason but a true one—is that it reflects the new form of government we have been living under for forty years—what we might call the Fourth Republic.

Maybe I exaggerate. But I think there is a connection between the meanness and irrationality of litigation now and the political wars that have been raging at the top. We engage in punch and smash mouth the way our leaders do. In court, we bash each other and rip into each other's private lives the way our media do.

Lawyers start to behave like talk-show hosts on radio.

And it's been my fate to be a lawyer in this "Fourth Republic." Let me explain the term. Some years ago, a Yale law professor, Bruce Ackerman, argued in a book, *We the People: Foundations* (1991) that the United States has had three "foundings," or three different types of republic. The first was in 1787, the second began after the Civil War, and the third came with the New Deal. In Ackerman's view, we've had three Constitutions, too, though unlike the Founders or Lincoln, the New Dealers did little formal amending of the Constitution.

I am fond—maybe too fond—of this tripartite way of understanding our history: we have had not one, not two, but three republics; and now, without any burst of trumpets, I think we are living in the Fourth Republic.

And it's a weak, unstable kind of republic, like the Fourth Republic for France. It's a republic of a permanently divided government; when one party has the Congress, the other usually has the White House. And the Court is permanently divided too. Until lately in our history, we had long periods where only one party or other ran the government. That is, only one party controlled the Congress, the presidency, and the Supreme Court. Long ago, Arthur Schlesinger Sr. made the argument that this was the natural case—he called it the Cycles of American History, as if these cycles of one-party dominance might roll on eternally.

Then suddenly, the cycles of American history stopped. Yes, from 2000 to 2006, the Republican Party had more control than usual, but it never had real control of the Senate, where it needed sixty votes. It also never had the Supreme Court.

Now as I write, we are back to our full-blown unstable divided government again.

And, of course, I did not think up this idea of divided government all by myself. My old college professor, S, did. But it does explain a lot: At a constitutional level, the leaders of our country have begun to behave like litigants in court—or I should say, *out* of court, in the way we brutalize people in discovery or depositions.

In our time, instead of check and balance, we went to punch and smash. Congress versus president, Democrat versus Republican, left versus right—it's hard for the Constitution to work when there is a two-party deadlock that no true majority can form to break. Since neither party can get a majority in the proper or lawful way, both are tempted to try extraconstitutional or even lawless ways to get control. Since 1970, here are just a few of these new extraconstitutional tactics.

- The use of a special prosecutor, even one who has lately threatened Bush
- Two uses of Congressional impeachment

- The hunting of President Reagan, in Iran-Contra
- The Supreme Court decision to stop the count in *Bush v. Gore*
- The recent semi-official attempts to keep African Americans from going to the polls

It's as if we went from contract to tort in a constitutional sense, or in settling which branch of the government is bigger and more important than the other. At different times, depending on which party controlled which branch, each side came up with one extraconstitutional hammer blow to use against the other.

Meanwhile, as more people drop out, it is harder for a majority to form to bring the deadlock to an end. Besides, the voting rate is the least of it. To an extent, as 2000 and 2004 have shown, one can keep the presidential voting rate up to 55 or 60 percent, literally by spending an extra $4 billion or more. In the congressional election, we even got a turnout of 40 percent, now a remarkably high figure. How much longer the extra multibillion-dollar infusion can keep it pumped up that high is unclear. As I write, many evangelicals have started to say, "We've had it." The turnout in the primaries has been dropping. While we can bully a bare majority to vote, most people have stopped paying attention. Fewer read the papers: circulation is dropping at a rate of 2 percent to 10 percent a year. Fewer even watch the news—yes, even Fox News's audience is tiny, maybe a tenth of that for a show like *Survivor* or *American Idol.*

I admit, it's all complicated. As college students know, everything in life is multifaceted. But the voting rate, or I would say the civic-attention rate, is far lower here than in other countries. One reason may be that our major political institutions are becoming less accountable.

First, the Senate is less accountable. Since a change in Senate rules in 1976, it now typically requires 60, not 50 votes to pass a law. Why go out and vote for change if the Senate can't respond to it?

Second, the House is less accountable. It is so gerrymandered now that the United States has to lose a war for even a handful of Congressional seats to change. Pundits talk about the "huge impact" of Iraq in the 2006 elections. What is astonishing is the small impact of Iraq in state after state: thanks to gerrymandering, for example, there was virtually no impact in Texas, despite the war, the Tom DeLay scandal, and many other horrors.

Third, the president is less accountable. It seems people now vote for president in just two or three battleground states. The rest of us, in a sense, can just phone in our votes. Besides, the president has lost much of his power. He is easier to impeach, to prosecute. He is less able to enforce the law. Though my friends are aghast when I say it, I think even Bush in his first six years has been weak.

Bush did manage to start a war. But otherwise a president in a divided government does less and less. Why bother to vote if a president can do so little?

Fourth, the Supreme Court is less accountable. At least it is less moored to Footnote Four and the goal of "more participation." Indeed, for the right-wing Justices, including Roberts and Alito, the less we participate, the more they like it. After all, they owe their appointments to *Bush v. Gore*.

Perhaps I overstate the argument. But let me say a little more about each of these four points.

The Senate

When I passed the bar in Washington, D.C., in 1975, it took a simple majority of senators to pass a bill. Any child knew that.

Now no one knows, or at least knows the answer on any given bill. Strangely, whether a bill takes fifty or sixty votes to pass is up to a minority of senators to decide. In 1976, the Senate "streamlined" and "improved" the old racist filibuster, which took two-thirds of the Senate to break. Now, after the reform, it takes only three-fifths. Wasn't that better? No, it was worse. By 1976, the old filibuster was already dead, or so disreputable that no one dared to use it. It was the equivalent of waving the Confederate flag. Senators were blushing. Until 1976, the filibuster was used on rare occasions, for the meanest, most racist reasons: say, to stop the government from regulating the Ku Klux Klan, or doing anything to stop white people from murdering blacks. So why would anyone want to reform it?

Well, to stop the government from passing useful laws. It is hard to imagine that the deregulation of law could have gone so far in the country without the improvement and increased use of the filibuster, also known as the sixty-vote rule. But when it happened in 1976, the story barely even made it into the papers.

Even without the supermajority rule, the Senate is monstrously unaccountable. Or let's say it is accountable to an imaginary country that has stolen the identity of the real United States. The reason is this: every one of the fifty states gets the same two Senate seats. When there were only thirteen states, this may have been a harmless thing. To be sure, Madison and Hamilton seethed about it, since it skewed the principle of one person, one vote. Maybe they knew that in just a few years Abbé Sieyès would squawk. But the way our *fifty* states now skew the principle of one person, one vote through the medium of the Senate is far worse than the way of the original thirteen. To see what I mean, pick up the flight magazine of American Airlines and look at the U.S. map to see the red dots where all the airports are. Really, the United States consists of three big clusters of red dots, and then a lot of empty space. The three red-dot clusters are (1) California, (2) Texas, and (3) east of the Mississippi old USA. The rest is white—empty space.

What's in all that empty space?

Senators. That's where they come from. States with no red dots, and hardly any people—that's how a group of senators representing only 9 percent of the population can theoretically be enough to block a bill.

But to put it that way invites this retort: "Well, you think there is some big difference between big and small states. Why do they have such different interests? The small states don't vote as a bloc."

But the evil is not Big versus Small, but Region versus Region, or North versus South, or Slave versus Free, or Blue versus Red, or Energy Producer versus Energy Consumer. The evil is not that in theory 10 percent can block 90 percent, but that in the real world 25 percent can and do block 75 percent.

With such a ratio, the country is schizophrenic. On the one hand, there is the real America. On the other, there is the faux America, where Wyoming has as many people as New York—except it doesn't. But it's this faux America to which the U.S. Senate reports. And over time the real America is the country that the faux America allows. It decides if we ratify Kyoto or if the polar ice caps melt. The result is, America doesn't make any sense to itself.

People say, "But the senate is so neat, and I just love Hillary Clinton and Barack Obama. . . ." I like them too. I'm not proposing to get rid of the Senate. To the contrary, if we had only one chamber, as in Britain, things might be even worse. But if the Senate is not based on one person, one vote, or modified in some way by proportional representation, then we get the faux America we have, a country that is always a stranger to itself.

If we had one person, one vote in the Senate, for example, we would have passed labor law reform not once but twice: Jimmy Carter had a bill that passed the House, but not the Senate, thanks to a filibuster. Bill Clinton had another bill that also passed the House, but not the Senate, again thanks to a filibuster.

If not for the Senate, we would be a European social democracy. If that's what the real America wants, then let America be America. Let a simple majority rule. Otherwise, voters will keep dropping away.

The House

In the long run, the country might be stabler if at least the House were based on one person, one vote—but it's not.

"The political scientists think the biggest problem in the country today is the gerrymandering of the House," says my friend Peter Levine, a political scientist. It is true the Democrats won despite the gerrymandering; but they also won because of it. After all, the Democrats have safe seats as well.

Indeed, because the House is so gerrymandered, even racially, it limits the kind of political leaders who can emerge. Because of the way the congressional map is gerrymandered in Illinois, Barack Obama probably could never have won a House seat. In some districts, he would be "too black," and not "black enough" in others.

There's another way gerrymandering hurts the Democrats, especially. The larger the electorate, the better it is for the Democrats. But gerrymandering makes elections less competitive, and holds down the number of voters who might identify with the Democrats. Also, if the House were more in play, the Republicans might start to move a bit more to the left.

After the 2006 election, it may be easier to scoff at the evils of gerrymandering. But how could the Democrats ever have won but for the loss of the war? "All politics is local." That's a chilling thought, because the Democrats could take over the House only on a national issue, the war in Iraq. It shows how weak the party was, and still is, district by district, "locally," on the ground.

Besides, even the 2006 election, a "referendum on a military defeat," brought out only a few more voters than in the last off-year election, four years before. It is amazing the number of House seats that remained perfectly safe, especially in Texas, home of the Tom DeLay scandal. The bigger the state, like Texas, the better gerrymandering works: there are more ways to slice-and-dice the races. That's true nationally too. There are more ways to gerrymander the same 435 seats in a nation of 300 million than there were fifty years ago in a nation of 230 million.

Worse, thanks to the Supreme Court's decision to back gerrymandering in *League of United Latin American Citizens v. Perry* (2006), it's now possible to recarve up the state of Texas, or any other state, every two years. So while the Democrats may have won back the House, the right to gerrymander the House may be worse for us in the long run than the filibuster in the Senate. For one thing, as many op-ed pieces point out, it means that state legislatures elect the House indirectly by the way they draw up the congressional map of their states. Aside from the irony of such a thing for democratic theory, the really bad part is that so many state legislators are for sale. It's because the state parties are in control that the Congress is more corrupt.

About a year ago, I was so upset that, without anyone asking or wanting me to do it, I tried to file an amicus brief in one of the Perry cases—not in the Supreme Court, but at the trial level. Well, I was lucky to get in with a small group of Texas lawyers. At least we all kept our sense of humor.

Our legal argument, which was ignored, was simple, even obvious, though no one had ever presented it: namely, gerrymandering violates the First Amendment. It classifies people based on their political views. It not only classifies but moves them, literally, from one district to the next, for no other reason than simply how they vote. How does that violate the Constitution?

Imagine that the state of Texas decides to keep the lines of the district just the same but moves people physically to get the same result. Suppose one night when I'm at home watching *Survivor* instead of *Fox News*, a Texas Ranger knocks at my door: "I'm sorry, sir, but we have too many Democrats here in Waco. So we brought around a truck here to take your things to Lubbock. We want to set you up there in Lubbock because, you know, we want the ratio of Democrats to Republicans here to stay more or less the same."

I've got nothing against Lubbock, but why should I have to move just because there are too many Democrats in Waco? Gerrymandering is the same thing in a much more velvet way. Because there are too many Democrats in the first congressional district, I am "moved" over to the second. The only difference is that they don't pack up my belongings and haul me away.

That was our argument, which the court ignored, of course. Besides, even for the Democrats, it went too far. Both parties want to keep *some* gerrymandering.

The President

The president is also becoming less accountable. He's also weaker, with less of a role, with shorter coattails, and to help his party carry Congress. Gerrymandering is partly to blame. The lockup of the Electoral College also weakens a president's popular base. In four-fifths of the states, why bother to vote for president? Of course, thank God, some people still do. But thanks to the media and the pundits, it is now burned into people's brains that in most states, the election is already over. It takes place only in Ohio, Florida, and a few other states. Since a presidential candidate cannot increase the turnout in most states, it means that even a strong president today has much shorter coattails. It makes him less of a popular tribune.

The presidential voting rate, even at the new "high" of 55 to 60 percent, is one of the scandals of the world. With fewer voters coming out, and with Congress ever more gerrymandered, it's harder to bring in a new Congress. It's even arguable that it's not a president who brings in a new Congress, but a Congress that brings in a new President. It seems to me that part of the appeal of electing Bush and not Gore in 2000 was to end the standoff of the later Clinton years between the president and the Congress. That's why they elected Bush. One problem with this argument is that the people actually elected Gore. But the point is, it is easier to change a president than a gerrymandered House. At least in 2000 and 2004, the two major candidates for president seemed irrelevant and weak.

After thirty years of divided government, the presidency was weak. "That's Dick Cheney's argument," a friend of mine said. Well, it's true. It's ironic that Bush and Cheney have made the presidency even weaker. It may have been partly the hope of restoring the strong presidency of old that Bush and Cheney started the war. If nothing else worked, a war is usually a good way to pump up presidential power. The Civil War, World War II, even the cold war before détente set in—each of these made the president all powerful.

Of course if that was the idea, it's ended in disaster. It has cost them the Congress. Indeed, without the war, Bush and Cheney could have kept a pliable Congress and perhaps over time brought the presidency back.

I know my friends are aghast when I try to make this argument: that Bush started this war not because he was so strong but because he was so weak. Like a few others in history, or even today—in smaller countries in Africa, for example— Bush started the war to mobilize his base: to whip up people, to get the "mandate" that as the actual loser in the 2000 election he could not claim to have.

One way to whip up his base was, alas, to start breaking the law. It's what made Bush a hero to the new Jacobins, the kids in the Federalist Society—the ones who as a point of principle want to see a president who is not only more powerful but above the law. That's why it was so important for them that Bush claim the right to engage in torture. If he had the right to torture, to undo the Geneva Convention, then it would prove nothing was stable. "Oh, he's claiming the right to torture— the presidency is out of control." So my friends said.

But it was not the presidency itself that was out of control: it was this movement, this Jacobin movement, that was out of control. Bush has never been the full commander-in-chief of this movement. Sometimes, he seemed more like one of its detainees. When Bush nominated a Texas woman lawyer who was not in the club, the Federalists sneered at her and got Congress to withdraw her name. The people in this movement did not care about presidential power—or congressional power either. For them the legal controversies of the Iraq war were about showing how far they could "deregulate" the settled law.

Let's go back to how any president now is weaker and how this weakness has hurt the Rule of Law.

Domestic Policy

It seems the president is strong in domestic policy. Many were surprised how much Bush did in his first term when he had "no mandate." Look at the tax cuts, for example. How could he do it with no mandate? Well, the president may have had no mandate, but Congress did. Under Clinton, a right-wing Congress was desperate to cut taxes, but even when impeached, Clinton still stood in the way. After 2000, Clinton was gone. Stamping and fuming, Congress was like a pent-up racehorse. Bush was like the stable boy who opened up the gate. Other initiatives came from the Congress. Over Bush's protest, it was Congress that created the Department of Homeland Security. Also over Bush's protest, it was Congress that created a new intelligence bureaucracy, currently headed by John Negroponte. In effect, Congress told Bush who would brief him at breakfast.

Take almost any domestic issue, whether it is gasohol, or drug regulation, and follow the money: it's decided in the Congress. During George W. Bush's presidency, the number of registered lobbyists has tripled. It tripled to lobby Congress, not to fuss with Bush. Meanwhile the Congress defunded him. It shortchanged him even on Homeland Security. He is short of food inspectors, health inspectors, rail inspectors. He does not have enough guards to guard our ports and terminals. The times when Bush has looked like a bungler, it is often due to the fact that Congress defunded him. It's fair enough to say it did so to pay for the tax cut. Also Bush himself did not ask for more money. The defunding was often with his approval. Yet it comes down to the same thing—the presidency is weaker.

It is usually the case that Congress has the president in its grip. Even when the Congress seems to let go, it can stop a runaway president. It always has the purse—the power to tax and spend. Congress is always Dad, and the president is always Junior, who has to ask for the keys to the car. The Roundheads in Parliament are always stronger than the king and the Cavaliers. Bush seems strong, but it was partly because he came out of the party of the Roundheads—he was a Roundhead, a weak one, though people on the left mistook him for a Cavalier.

It is ironic that as the presidency shrank, a great claim was being made for an all-powerful president, a so-called unitary executive, who had "all" executive power. In reality, he lacks the money to execute the laws. First, in a country that has become more or less a corporate plutocracy, it has become harder for a president like Bush to recruit any good agency managers. In the Eisenhower era, and then in the Nixon-Ford era, the Republicans were famous for bringing in good managers—sometimes, to whip into shape liberal programs left in shambles by the Democrats. Nixon could bring in CEOs, or at least vice presidents. Today, how can a president like Bush afford them? In 1970, the forty top CEOs in the United States had an average pay of $1.3 million, and the corporate junior officers made much less. In 2004, however, the top forty had an average pay of well over $40 million a year, and even a mere head of human relations in one of these companies can now make up to $5 million a year. It's preposterous to think that Bush could get a reasonably talented personnel officer to give up $5 million a year to take a job as a manager at the Census Bureau for $140,000. No wonder he ends up with ne'er-do-wells like

Michael Brown at FEMA. It also forces him to use government lawyers, like Michael Chertoff, who never went into the private sector or billed at $850 an hour. But lawyers like Chertoff have no great abilities as managers. The result is, the government cannot seem to execute the basic plays. Think not just of the Katrina debacle, but of the 2004 shortfall in the flu vaccine, or the confusion in the sign-up for the Medicare drug benefit, or the minor comic moments such as the appointment of a veterinarian to take charge of women's health programs. So Bush and future presidents may have to use the army more and more: one day the military will end up running the drug program for Medicare. But even army officers—the talented ones, at least—are leaving for multimillion-dollar corporate jobs.

Meanwhile, even lower down the career ladder, Bush, like any president, does more and more contracting-out. This is true especially of security. In our firm we represent several hundred guards who guard federal buildings—they are the front line in the war on terror. But even they are not federal employees. They work for private contractors, who nickel-and-dime them on their wages and hold up their full pay (in our case) for over a year, in the same way we nickel-and-dime the army. It's a symptom of a weakened presidency, short of money, drained by a plutocracy that can manipulate the Congress.

It's the very opposite of the executive branch that Theodore Lowi imagined in his well-known book *The End of Liberalism*, which came out in 1969. He foresaw an all-powerful federal bureaucracy that would virtually ignore the Congress. Instead we live in a culture of K Street lobbyists who fasten on to the Congress and ignore the mediocrities and the also-ran's who merely run the programs.

Foreign Policy

Of course the president has more power in foreign policy. Yet even here in the last thirty years the presidency has become weaker. Under Bush, it is true there is—or was—much talk of a unitary executive. The theory put forward by the Federalists is that the president, or at least a Republican president, has all executive power, with no right by Congress even to question what he does. With a Democratic Congress the theory seems preposterous. It was preposterous under the Republican Congress as well. Things just don't work that way, in reality, under the Constitution, no matter how much right-wing lawyers might wish. Long ago Richard Neustadt of Harvard wrote that the Constitution provides not for the separation of powers but for a sharing of powers. Like it or not, Congress is involved in the execution of the laws and the making of foreign policy. Likewise, the president is part of the legislative process. It's obvious in domestic policy—does any lobbyist on K Street believe in the unitary executive? But it's also true in foreign policy. In a world that has more law of every kind that now links the nations—trade law, privacy law, criminal law—Congress has a bigger role in foreign policy than it has ever had in American history. The president can show up at photo-ops in India or Vietnam, but now he usually has to hold off the trip until the Congress approves a new trade agreement, or a nuclear information-sharing program, or some similar new law. More than before, in making any foreign policy, the president is under a tighter and tighter rein of Congress. And with the Senate so skewed away from one person, one vote, there is more and more that a president literally cannot do precisely because of Congress—or at least because of the requirement that an unrepresentative Senate must approve treaties by a two-thirds vote. A two-thirds vote might or might not be a rational threshold if the Senate itself were based on one person, one vote. But the hurdle is far too high, dangerously high, for the United States to function in the world. It may not make it literally impossible for the president to work together with other countries to take action against global warming. But it would be a shame if the planet Earth loses its last chance of survival because constituents in Wyoming and Utah object.

It is easier to get out of this constitutional deadlock if a president starts a war. He then has more freedom to maneuver in foreign policy—or at least he can get more congressional deference if he can appeal to the country as commander-in-chief. He has more freedom to make or break the laws. The Federalists and neoconservatives may or may not have been pursuing Wilsonian democratic ideals, but they were doing it in a way that fits an agenda of deregulating at home. The breakdown of law in one area helps in the breakdown of law in another.

Bush did get more deference because he started the war, but even so, it was only in limited areas. Yes, one could say, he got the right to torture; but in a sense, that's all he's got. Generally, except in this outlandish way, his presidency became weaker, even in foreign policy. He may reflect on this every morning when, against his wishes, he has to meet with Negroponte to be briefed.

In a sense, Bush's own claim, or his lawyers' claim, to be a unitary executive who can act without Congress may have made him weaker. When Bush claimed that he could act without the Congress, it meant he cut himself off from Congress. That meant he became a prisoner of his staff. Bush is a good example of a weak executive, too much in the grip of Cheney types and neocons who were pursuing their own agenda, and not necessarily looking after him. It was in Bush's interest—

in the interest of any president, as president—to bring in the Congress, and not to keep it out.

For biblical reasons, it is bad to call anyone a fool, but Bush has been a fool. He let the kids—the Clarence Thomas law clerks, the Federalists, the neocons—tell him that he could break the laws or, in a postmodern way, he could create his own reality. He cut himself off from people in Congress who might have told him what was going on.

The Court

If one branch loses power, it is in the nature of the Constitution that another branch will get it. As the presidency has lost power, the Court has found itself with more. My old college professor, S, disagrees. "You wouldn't say the Supreme Court plays a bigger role than it did in the 1930s when it tried to block the New Deal?" Yes, I would say so. Even in the 1930s the Court would not have had the nerve, by itself, to overturn the popular vote as it did in our time in *Bush v. Gore*—or do it the *way* the Court did, by taking the case away from the Florida Supreme Court and putting in different rules than the state courts would use. Nor could that old Court stop a president as the Supreme Court stopped Bush this summer, in *Hamden v. Rumsfeld*, from setting up special courts for the detainees. Or at least the Court can make *Bush v. Gore* or *Hamden* stick in a way the "old" Court, even the Court in *Brown v. Board of Education* would have had far more trouble doing. Maybe some disagree. Then at least consider the range of cases before the Court today, compared to the "old" Court of eighty or even fifty years ago: gay rights, gerrymandering, affirmative action, and other big cases that come not once a decade but all in one year's docket. Even when compared to the "activist" Warren Court, the Court now sees and handles more big cases: we're just numbed to it now, in a way we were not (yet) in the 1960s. The length of the confirmation hearings of each new Justice, no matter how qualified, is a measure of the way the Court is taking more and more power from the other two branches.

But while I think the Supreme Court itself is more powerful, I should have said to S that I was not speaking of just "the Court," but *all* the courts, *all* the federal judges, and now the many magistrates and senior status judges—the whole judicial branch. It's the judicial branch as a whole that has taken power from the Congress and the executive.

When Lowi wrote *The End of Liberalism* in 1969, he expected that the Congress would lose power. After all, there were more laws and more legal regulation. But he assumed this would lead to more power in the executive branch. He foresaw an elite with huge amounts of "discretion" given over by Congress to apply the laws as the elite in the executive branch— the "best and the brightest"—decided in their wisdom to do.

But instead of this legislative-type power seeping out from the Congress to the executive, it ended up in the judicial branch instead. Federal judges ended up making these decisions, a little like proconsuls of the Roman Empire out in the provinces applying Roman law. Though perhaps it was too early for Lowi to notice, the number of federal judgeships under Kennedy and Johnson started to explode. In 1962, for example, in the Chicago federal district courts, the total number of federal judges was only *six*. That's all—six judges. In the courthouse two blocks away from me, as I write, there are now, as follows:

Full-time federal judges: 23
Magistrate judges (essentially, federal judges who can
    try cases): 10

Senior-status judges (who may have bigger case loads
than some of the full-time judges in 1962): 9

It seems fair to count the magistrate judge—a new office,
like an "assistant" judge—as doing the same work as a full federal judge. Though supervised, the magistrates run discovery,
do settlements, write long legal opinions, and try civil cases,
sometimes more than the full judges do. Also, the senior-status
judges are more active in this post-Viagra era. In 1962, they
would have been having two-martini lunches. So I'd say that in
terms of work being done, the number of judge equivalents
has gone up in the last few decades by a multiple of six or even
seven. In the executive or legislative branch, there's been no increase like that. Try to imagine the number of new federal
agency heads or members of Congress going up a multiple of
even two, much less six or seven.

And I am only considering the federal courts in Chicago.
The rate of increase is surely much higher in Los Angeles,
Washington, D.C., not to mention Miami, Dallas, and higher-
growth areas. Meanwhile, as judgeships and the rest grow,
many of the old New Deal administrative agencies have
literally disappeared. While the civilian federal work force
may have dropped, the number of perky young law clerks has
gone up.

Whether there is judicial "activism," there is certainly more
activity—men and women deciding more cases under more
laws. But that's a choice that both the right and the left made
together. During the period of divided government, the Republicans fought to increase judgeships too. Both the right and
left chose, on purpose, to govern the United States through
judges rather than with experts or specialists in the executive
branch. But judicial activism, on the whole, is much worse for

the left than the right. During the Warren Court era, the liberals came to see judges as purer, more moral, less corrupt, not sullied by special interests, as the old New Dealers were. The left came to prefer the Warren Court to the New Deal model. After all, from 1968 through 1994, the Democrats more or less held the Congress and the Republicans held the executive branch. It made more sense to let the judiciary enforce the law rather than set up another federal agency that Nixon or, even worse, Reagan would control. But the old New Deal model works much better than the Warren Court model as a way of regulating people in groups. It works better as a way of keeping a balance of power between unions, associations, corporate interests. The federal judges can't do this. They aren't experts. What they know is procedure. What they like best is not to make decisions at all but to knock out cases on procedural grounds—cases about drug prices or the environment or a host of other matters that they know nothing at all about except what they may read on a Sunday in the *New York Times.*

It's strange, then, when the right complains of judicial activism. On the whole, the right has the greater interest—or greater than the left's—in choosing judicial rather than presidential government. As an alternative to government by the executive, the increase in judicial activism, or activity, means that ultimately we end up regulating less. The Federalists are perfect for using the judicial model for carrying out this agenda: "What do we know about this area? The courts should hesitate to intervene," they say.

After 1960, in law after law, Congress authorized the federal courts to do the enforcing, rather than turn the matter over to an agency. Then, in opinion after opinion that I have had to read over the years, there is often this mock tone of surprise that this or that case has somehow come before the court—as if this were an affront to the judiciary, or they have been put upon in some way.

In fact, the only reason so many new and extra judges have gotten their glorious lifetime appointments is that the United States decided to let them sort out all these cases. It's also good that so many of them are so bright. Yet this continued mock surprise at having to do what they were appointed to do is tiresome.

Contrary to what Lowi or David Halberstam expected in the 1960s, the "best and brightest" now go to the judicial branch, not the executive. No doubt, even the old Supreme Court had wonderful clerks. Who would not want to clerk for Louis Brandeis? But in 1950, kids did not fight to be district or appellate court clerks in the carnivorous way they do today.

The young sense, or know, that the federal courts count far more than federal agencies now do. In an era of deregulation federal judges end up not with less power but with even more. The more unsettled the law is, the more discretion they have to shape it. As the last mandarins of the executive branch are pensioned off, as ever more of their work is privatized, the number of federal judges keeps rising. A new demand for government-by-judiciary brought forth new sources of supply. In our time, the Federalist Society became the big new feeder farm of federal judges. So even on the right, they want as many or more judges as we do on the left. In that sense, judicial activism, or activity (to use a neutral term), is a source of patronage that helps to hold the Republican coalition together.

The problem (or the crisis) is this: the kinds of judges who get into office, especially on the right, owe their appointments directly or indirectly to the fact that relatively fewer people vote or participate. In one way or the other, many on the right owe their appointments not to the fulfilment but to the frustration of Footnote Four. And it would be a natural interest or tendency of these judges to keep the country in a state of low turnout or divided government, or at least to not disturb the deadlock that allowed them to come to power.

In other words, judges on the right are readier to renounce politely (as with Roberts, mumbling about minimalism) or loudly (as with Scalia, giving the finger) what Harlan Stone's law clerk asked judges in a democracy to do. It's in the interest of judges on the right that not more but fewer people vote. And not just not vote, but not participate, not go to school, literally and figuratively, to get the skills of citizens.

For example, as a young lawyer, Roberts made his mark arguing that the states can keep children of undocumented parents out of the public schools. Fortunately, in *Plyler v. Doe,* his side lost. But Roberts seems to have been a true believer; it helped get him backing on the right. What can be better for the republic than to keep the poor out of schools? As a young lawyer, Alito was even worse. Long after most lawyers had stopped, he was still arguing against Reynolds and one person, one vote, even when there was no hope of going back. Yet Roberts and Alito are almost moderates compared to what Thomas and Scalia would do.

Many law professors seem to find the activism of the far right to be quirky, with no pattern or principle to what they do. It's not states' rights; it's not anything. Yes, it is erratic, and I love to make this same point. But in darker moments, I feel certain that there is a connecting thread: less participation. Put another way, it is not only that the Court, like Congress or the president, is less accountable to the people. Rather, the right-wing justices on it actually want to make the Court, and government generally, less accountable to the people.

Footnote Four is still the compass—only, they want to go in reverse.

Of course, it seems unfair—not to say painful—to bring up

Bush v. Gore. It's weird how, even on the left, lawyers shy away from discussing it. We all want to forget. ("It didn't really happen, did it?") The other day, in great excitement, a lawyer friend was saying to me: "*Hamden v. Rumsfeld*, I'm sure it'll turn out to be the most important single decision of our lifetimes." Wait—more important than *Bush v. Gore?* But of course he had suppressed it. After all, the Supreme Court told us even at the time to put it out of our heads. "Never cite this case again," the Court said, more or less. In a trance since 2000, many of us lawyers have hypnotically behaved, as if in an old Japanese science-fiction movie, with a title something like *The Day the Law Stood Still.*

Even if everyone were to keep shushing me, I'd still like to go on talking about *Bush v. Gore,* not because I'm still mad about it, but because it may be the Court's signature case. *Bush v. Gore,* the one we are "not allowed to cite," the stone the builders rejected, or at least said they would never use again, turns out to be the cornerstone of the legal system we're in.

"Shush! Don't say that."

But I do say that. The point of *Bush v. Gore* is to put down Footnote Four. The principle, if that's the word, is to keep the electorate as small as possible, to make it easier for the Federalists and their friends not just to become judges but to go on deregulating the law.

Whenever I think I should shush, I go back to what Scalia wrote when he stayed the recount of the vote. It still haunts me. Why should the Court have to issue an emergency stay of a recount permitted by the Florida Supreme Court under Florida state law? The reason, wrote Scalia, is that the recount would "threaten irreparable harm to petitioner [Bush] . . . by casting a cloud upon what he claims to be the legitimacy of the election." Yes, the "harm" is that all of us would find out if

Bush really won, and of course that would "cast a cloud" when he took office, as Scalia seems to assume that Bush would do—whether he really won the election or not. Even when the colonels in Latin American countries toss out elections, they do it more sensitively than that. To say the least, no longer is the rationale for judicial review to "clear the channels of political change" or promote majority rule; in fact, the new role is to stop us all from finding how the election came out!

Scalia and a few of us insiders may know this is no longer a democracy—but it would be irreparable harm if the entire nation knew.

It's true but too simple to say, "He did it because he's a Republican." He also did it because he's a judge, one who wants to put his imprint on the Court, to appoint the very person who would appoint the Court. If *Bush v. Gore* had gone the other way, there would inevitably have been a recount of the entire state vote, though Gore did not ask for it at first. That would have been the natural dynamic, which the Court cut off so that Bush could win. Without *Bush v. Gore*, Roberts and Alito would not be on the Court. So in a sense, in this case, the Court itself helped pick the future Court, or picked the president to pick it, in something like a judicial form of parthenogenesis.

One day a professor will write up a comparison between the Terry Schiavo law and the case of *Bush v. Gore*. Of course, one was an act of Congress, the other a Court case. But each was an act of God, a one-time intervention to rip away a case from the Florida state courts on an ad hoc legal basis made up on the spot because Republicans did not like how the case was coming out. In both cases, the idea was to reinsert the feeding tubes to keep alive someone or something that in the natural course of things simply would have died.

Of course Terry's Law was stopped; *Bush v. Gore* was not.

. . .

It's poisoned everything—and the effect of this poison will last for years. It certainly made it hard, if not impossible, to ever again invoke Footnote Four. So I should have known better to bring a right-to-vote case, in which all I did was argue a theory based on Footnote Four. I tell this story with tears in my eyes.

For two years after *Bush v. Gore,* I brooded about a law in my own state, Illinois. This ancient law prohibits people from voting "absentee" by mail. Only if you have to go "out of the county" in your horse and buggy, could you vote by mail. Now millions of commuters here were "out of the county" because every day they zip across a county line every ten minutes out on the tollways. But back in the central city, where people don't tend to cross county lines but are just as busy as their commuting fellow citizens, people would have to lie if they wanted the convenience of voting by mail. It was unfair! Besides, my clients wouldn't lie. So I brought a case for four of them—all working mothers, with tiny kids, full-time jobs, no babysitter. One of the moms was also going to school at night. She had even asked an election official: "Can I vote absentee?"

No. Not unless she was going to be absent from the county. Was she?

"Oh, come on," my friends said. "What's the problem? Everybody lies."

So I brought the case, pointed out the increase in working hours, the longer commute, the single-parent problem, and all sorts of difficulties with a law passed before there were cars, or indeed, before the mother of a child had the right to vote. Didn't the equal protection clause, which had been used by the majority in *Bush v. Gore* to override majority rule, actually require the state of Illinois to give these poor working mothers an equal right to vote?

Yes, I actually argued *Carolene Products.* I took the chance.

A little voice inside me said, "Don't do it." In the current legal climate, our side should play defense. I hear older lawyers tell younger ones, "Don't bring such a stupid case, you'll end up making bad law. Don't do it."

Oh, but I was sure I knew what I was doing. I was sure that if I could get before three judges and give my oral argument, they would blush and go my way. They would give these poor working mothers a chance to cast their votes.

To my shock, a newspaper reporter even ran a story in the *Chicago Tribune*. There was a terrific picture of my client, Ms. Julie, as she was standing in a gas station and pumping her own gas with her kids in the car.

By the way, I also alleged that the political machines were using this law to skew the vote. While honest people did not lie and say they would be "out of the county," many precinct captains told their people not to worry. They even went around urging "their people" to vote absentee so they would have time to fill out the bottom of the ballot for sewer commissioner.

How could I lose? On a motion to dismiss, a court has to take my allegations as true. I had these poor but honest moms who were crying out for a chance to vote by mail, and I had alleged massive fraud by the party machines rounding up all the voters who would lie.

How could I lose a motion to dismiss where a court assumes that what I'm saying is true?

Of course I did lose, and then I was foolish enough to appeal. If Footnote Four was barely alive, my case practically ended its life. The court held that if the state of Illinois wanted to "restrict voting opportunities" for any plausible reason, then the courts should just defer. The opinion came out a few weeks before the 2004 election. I had nightmares of it being cited in Ohio and Florida. But what about all the logic of Footnote Four? After all, if people like the working moms could not vote, then they could not change a law that kept working moms from voting. Here was a dream case for intervention by a federal court since the "majoritarian process" clearly can't work. The working people who cannot vote on Tuesday are not able to elect legislators who would let them vote on other days than Tuesday. Isn't that logical? What could the Court of Appeals say to such an argument?

It did not have to say anything. Judges don't have to answer my rhetorical questions.

And what about the fraud I alleged?

Well, I should let it go. But I still think about that case. In oral argument one judge said that the state of Illinois was the most corrupt state in the country. But then in the opinion, the court said that it would defer to the state of Illinois when it came to fighting fraud. Here the state claimed that the best way to fight fraud was only to let people vote if they were going "out of the county."

I still want to go back and cry out to them: "But why are you deferring to the most corrupt state in America as to the best way to fight corruption?"

I was so sure I could make sense of Footnote Four to three rational and reasonable people, as I truly believe these three judges to be. Yet they ignored my argument. In my head I kept repeating this line: whatever the states do to restrict voting opportunities for any rational reason, the courts should just defer. What could be worse for Footnote Four?

For the next few weeks, as the 2004 election came closer, I lost sleep over this case. I expected district courts in Ohio and Florida to cite it. It would all be my fault. How could I have been so stupid as to bring this case and make such rotten law?

But, of course, to get so upset was another act of narcissism. In fact, in neither Ohio nor Florida did any district court cite my case when after the election various civil rights and other groups brought challenges to the voting arrangements in those states. By the way, in Florida the federal district court threw out the case; the claim was that in the white and wealthy parts of the state, there were no lines, no problems with voting. In the poor and African American areas, there were shabby facilities, long lines, and massive problems voting. What was the federal district court's rationale? Too bad. But the Ohio district court sustained a similar claim, brought by the League of Women Voters. The Ohio case is now on appeal.

Even more encouraging, a Georgia federal court threw out a Georgia law that required a special new state-approved voter card in order to vote.

And most encouraging of all, Illinois adopted a law that allowed for in-person early-election voting, so it was possible at last for my four working moms to vote. It was not the solution we wanted, but at least they can vote on a weekend. So there was a happy ending to my story. Okay, I had been reckless to bring a suit like this. But at least there is a chance for working people to vote on a day other than Election Day itself.

However, there is a little problem with the new Illinois law. As it turns out, there are no legal standards for a fair and even distribution of the early-election polling places. So in the first election under the new law, the Democratic machine set up early-election polling sites in all the machine wards. They had not a single polling place on the Lakefront, where all the anti-machine independents are.

It's a perfect case for Footnote Four. That's why I've brought a suit. Don't worry. This time I have co-counsel, and he's much smarter. Anyway, the real right-to-vote battle is not up here but in the South.

CHAPTER 14

The Case
Against Civilization

In the Supreme Court's 2006 term, Justice Kennedy seemed to have made a kind of "Sophie's choice." In 2006, he cast the swing vote in the five-to-four decision in *Hamdan v. Rumsfeld*, the case knocking out Bush's plan for special tribunals, to be set up outside even *military* law. These drumhead tribunals would have tried detainees like Hamdan for the crime of conspiracy, and would have deprived them even of the right to see or rebut certain secret evidence that they had ever been in a conspiracy. It was pretty Orwellian. By only one vote, though, did the Court strike down these special courts, and only because Bush would have to get the approval of Congress. Four Justices did say that the plan to try Hamdan with secret evidence he could not see or rebut would deprive him of "all the guarantees . . . recognized as indispensable by civilized peoples," as set out in Common Article 3 of the Geneva Conventions.

As the fifth, or swing, vote, Justice Kennedy would not go so far—he would not say that the use of secret evidence would cheat Hamdan of "all the guarantees . . . recognized as indispensable by civilized peoples." Still, to the outrage of Federalist types, he did vote to scrap the tribunals and make Bush go back to Congress.

But he was the swing vote in the other great case I cared about: *League of United Latin American Citizens v. Perry*, the case that upheld Tom DeLay's 2003 special law gerrymandering Texas to elect more congressional Republicans. This time Kennedy swung to the right. Even though it took place in the middle of the decade, and even though Texas Rangers had to track down Democrats to drag them to the state house to get a quorum, the Court upheld the plan. Of course, the Federalist types were elated.

Yet Kennedy seems ready to bash gerrymandering. Or so it seems from a recent past opinion. I think he hated joining Scalia and others in upholding the way DeLay had carved up Texas in 2003. But it's my wild and unsupportable guess that he told himself, late one night, alone in his study:

"Heck, I can't vote with the 'liberals' on both *Hamdan* and *Perry*. My old friends on the right would be too mad. Look how they yelled about Blackmun when he broke ranks. The crazies began stalking him. And look at David Souter, when he wrote that opinion on eminent domain. Didn't they picket his house? What would they do to me?"

So he could only do one, *Hamdan* or *Perry*. He could either cast a vote in favor of civilization (strike down the secret courts in *Hamdan*) or cast a vote in favor of democracy (strike down the gerrymandering of Congress in *Perry*). But he could not do both, or the Federalists would say, "He's another Souter, or even a Blackmun." And he shrank at the thought that they'd all begin to scream.

So he voted in favor of civilization, and not democracy. What would you have done if you had had to choose?

I told my theory about Kennedy's choice to a co-counsel in

Session v. Perry, which was a related case. (As I said, we had
filed our humble amicus in the lower court.) "For Kennedy," I
said, "it was civilization or democracy."

"Too bad that he picked the wrong one," he said.

"You're right," I said. "He made the wrong choice."

Even in *Hamdan*, what happened? After the Court struck
down Bush's plan, it sent it back to Congress, a Congress that
had been gerrymandered by DeLay and others. Congress then
took Bush's plan and *did* make it better—but also made it
worse. Congress did stop the use of secret evidence—a good
thing, to be sure. But then Congress stripped the detainees of
any right to habeas corpus review.

By stopping such review, Congress tried to make sure there
would never be another *Hamdan*. Before the Democrats won in
2006, it used to baffle me that liberals wanted the Congress to
straighten out Bush on Guantánamo. "The Congress has to
act," and so forth. Why? When a president acts abusively, at least
he cannot strip the Supreme Court literally of *jurisdiction*, the
power even to decide cases about such abuses in the future.

That's what a pro-Bush Congress was likely to do—and did.
So why get a pro-Bush Congress to bless at least part of what
Bush was up to in Guantánamo and then strip the Court of the
very power to decide such cases in the future? Oh, yes, *Hamdan*
is a great decision. But in terms of advancing our civilization,
one can question what Kennedy and the others really got.

But even if that weren't true, it still seems to me he made the
wrong choice. He came out in favor of civilization over democracy. By his one vote, we missed a chance to hold the Congress
accountable.

Of course, we should always come out in favor of "civilization." Down at the University of Chicago, there are even some
in law or economics who would come out in favor of civiliza-

tion, or at least up to a point. Don't misunderstand—I think our country already is a great civilization. But it is a great civilization because it is a democracy. That's our special contribution to civilization. It's our democracy that civilizes us.

Let's suppose I am the law clerk of a certain Mr. Justice K. I knock on his door, though it's late at night. He's still reading briefs. Anyway, he's been sleepless, even haunted, ever since he voted with the majority in *Bush v. Gore*. When I walk in, he asks me my opinion, as to whether he should go with civilization or democracy.

I start to blubber about democracy, blah-blah-blah.

"Cut it out," he says. "Look at these poor wretches down in Guantánamo. They're probably being tortured, tonight, right now. And you want me to go chasing after Tom DeLay? What will that accomplish? Oh, sure, let's have more 'participation.' Let's 'democratize' the country. Look, no court is going to 'democratize' this country. I see the kids your age, my God, they give me the creeps. I don't mean the clerks, of course—though some of them give me the creeps, but that's different. No, I mean the kids out there in the fake Irish bars, in all the Starbucks, out there in Atlanta, in L.A., I mean, all over. I bet half of them have never read a paper. They couldn't follow a news story. They have no opinions. They don't know who Tom DeLay is, or care. They just put on their iPod, they hit something. Click. In any civic sense, they're out of here. We're never going to hear from them again. You think some court is somehow going to yank off those headphones? There's nothing we can do."

If I'm his law clerk, he wants me to argue. So here's what I say.

"Okay, Judge, I see your point, but you know, you're selling us all a little short, aren't you? If you want to bring us back, you have to give us some kind of role. Though I'm not sure what it is, you have to give us something to *do*. Take the New Deal, and all that—all the old type of regulation. That's never going to come back. And what we've got to replace it, all these federal judges, seven hundred or so, and all the magistrates, trying to run things—that's not working, either. There's got to be something to go in its place. What? There's got to be some way to give people something to do."

Of course I should say: Why do you have to make a choice? Even so, I'd go after the gerrymandering first.

How do I know for sure that if there were "more participation," there would be more civilization? I don't. But if the prison rate is a measure of civilization, I think it's rational to believe that the prison rate would decline.

I say that just because where participation rates are higher (voting, reading the paper, unionization, work councils), the prison rate is lower, often drastically lower. Indeed, when our participation rates were higher, the prison rate used to be much lower here. It's no coincidence that we not only imprison people more but keep them from voting. We "criminalize" a significant portion of the electorate. If we did not lock up so many people in prison in Florida and then deny them the right to vote—over half a million people—George Bush would not have become president in 2000. A half-million disenfranchised voters in just one state may seem like a small number. Yet it's a big enough number, in not just an "electoral" but a moral sense, to change the history of our country.

The same term that the Supreme Court decided *Hamdan* about the rights of Guantánamo detainees, it let stand another decision about detainees in Florida. It was the decision of the U.S. Court of Appeals for the Eleventh Circuit in *Johnson v. Bush*—that Florida has the right to bar six hundred thousand ex-felons from voting. If these Florida ex-felons, or ex-detainees, had had the right to participate in the political process, at least in the 2000 election, the Supreme Court in *Hamdan* would never have had to invoke the Geneva Conventions and international human rights.

One reason we argue over international or human rights law is that we keep so many people from the polls at home. In law schools, the students study the Geneva Conventions. But who reads the text of the Fourteenth Amendment? Two thirds of it is the Penalty Clause, and few if any lawyers even know it exists. The Penalty Clause says that if a state excludes eligible citizens from voting in any way, it should lose a proportionate number of electoral votes. While it has a proviso for those involved in "rebellion or other crime," it is supposed to be applied narrowly, and it should not apply to the over 600,000 (mainly black) Americans barred as ex-felons from voting at all in Florida. If we had invoked the Penalty Clause in Florida before 2000, Bush would never have been elected President. We would now be peacefully complying with the Geneva Conventions.

As I write this, Florida's new governor is considering an executive order to let the ex-felons have their full voting rights. It just shows that there can be good news for those who still hope for a functioning republic

Meanwhile, what shocks me as a labor lawyer is the way we "criminalize" the electorate, or at least disenfranchise so many U.S. hourly workers. Here I think not just of the millions of ex-felons but the so-called illegal aliens. Call them what you please, but these are now a big fraction of the hourly workers of America. They live here, work here, and pay taxes. "But they're not citizens!" They certainly are, for GDP purposes. They are citizens so far as the economy is concerned. If they can't vote, it cuts down the power of working people to raise their wages. An economist friend of mine says, "The percentage of hourly versus salaried people hasn't changed for years."

So if fewer of the people holding hourly jobs can vote, it means the Democrats lose more of their traditional base. It also makes it harder to raise the minimum wage. It makes it easier, in our politics, for the rich to take from the poor.

It's hard to say whether immigration has driven down the "market" wage, or depressed wages in a purely economic sense. But it's obviously helped hold down or drive down the "political" wage, or the statutory minimum wage. If more and more hourly workers can't vote, they are weaker politically. This is true even though the share of hourly workers in the economy is as great as ever.

That's why "disenfranchised" immigration has tipped the political balance of power, not just between right and left, but between haves and have-nots. It's not immigration but disenfranchisement. It's a point that Thomas Jefferson or James Madison would have seen easily, but it's hard for many of us to see. It's this criminalization, or disenfranchisement, of the electorate that has helped drive up the increase in the prison population. If more of the low-income population could vote, we would not be locking up so many of them. Worse, by the late 1990s, we had more people who were "illegal" in another sense: I mean the ex-welfare moms, the ex-felons, the hustlers, and the working poor who work "off the books" in a vast underground economy. One way to survive in low-wage America is to find a job in the back of a shop where neither "boss" nor "employee" pay any taxes. By ending welfare as we know it, we ended up with a bigger part of our electorate now living underground, at least so far as the IRS is concerned. It's helped, of course, that the IRS, underfunded as it is, is collapsing too. As more people are pulled into living outside the law, the last thing they will do is "surface" themselves by registering to vote.

Without fixing this electoral problem, without "more participation," I doubt the Supreme Court or any other elite could do much to stop or curb the huge power of "Prison," this whole secret government which has sprung up. Let's put aside whether, in the name of civilization, the Supreme Court could do anything much about prison conditions or impose its will on all the sheriffs, police, prison guards, security companies, and the like. Lately, when the Court has been in the mood to be humane, it's had trouble imposing its will even on the lower federal courts. For example, in the November 14, 2004, edition of the *New York Times*, a front-page story reported on the Fifth Circuit's refusal to carry out a direct order from the Supreme Court as to how to review a death penalty case. By an eight-to-one vote, the Supreme Court sent a Texas case back to the Fifth Circuit to review it under a slightly more "pro-defendant" standard. The Fifth Circuit refused: they wanted to follow the lone Clarence Thomas dissent.

It seems that in the South there are federal appellate judges who find every Justice on the Court—Scalia, Rehnquist, and everyone but Thomas—just too liberal to stomach. That's why there are not only so many in prison, but prison conditions in the United States are so harsh.

The only way to attack this problem of our civilization is the indirect way—by expanding participation, by restoring a political balance of power, if not to reduce, then at least to check the growth in prisons over the next ten to twenty years. We need Footnote Four more than ever.

A reader who skipped the preceding chapter might well say, "But why are you always talking about the courts? Why not leave this to the legislature, the Senate and the House?" Well, read the preceding chapter. But there's another, less flippant answer: the ultimate goal of Footnote Four is to leave everything to the legislature—even to our less-than-representative Senate and our gerrymandered House. But we can't leave them the last

word on how many of us get to participate when we have crim-
inalized so much of the electorate and rigged so many of the
rules. At any given time, the legislators are those who benefit
from these rules. Even the Democrats who just won got to where
they are under the existing rules. With a little tweaking, perhaps, many of them are probably content with the rules just the
way they are. On the left, some even *like* the existing rules. I can
testify from personal experience that even on the left there are
community groups, advocacy groups, that don't especially want
"more participation," even if they say they do. They have
"their" lists and "their" people, and they only want "certain"
people, "our" people, the "right" people to participate.

And if there's a single reason not to rely on the legislature,
it's been the way the legislatures have handled the funding
of the public schools. Not a single legislature, on its own, has
done anything to stop the use of the local property tax to short-
change the kids from the poorest districts. What better way
to keep the poor from "more participation"? In every case of
reform, it was a state supreme court that had to step in.

That's why any strategy to democratize the country depends
on the courts.

Of course, the legislature is important too: indeed, we need
a legislature in order to check the courts. After all, people also
need more trust in the Rule of Law, in the legal process. Then
they might see more point in participating in the political
process. It's not one or the other of these two approaches; it's
both of them at once.

"That's fine," a reader may say. "But what exactly do we do?
I'd like to see a plan."

Well, it happens that I have a plan.

CHAPTER 15

The Plan

First, we have to bring back predictability in the law. That means we have to move when and where we can from tort back to contract, from tort back to trust, from tort back to post–New Deal kind of administrative law or regulation. I think we have to start with the states: perhaps get one or two big states as models. Or get lawyers and judges to meet in their downtown clubs and adopt some "model laws," on everything from employment at will to credit cards, company arbitrations, and the like. Then get the club members who are the federal judges to leave these laws alone: "I know these guys from the clubs, so I'll cut these laws a little slack, and I won't hold that they're preempted."

It's my claim that in some of the states, some blue states, like Oregon, democracy really could work. On the whole, I think the lack of one person, one vote at the federal or national level holds down turnout even in the most progressive blue states. On the other hand, the fact of a lower turnout can make it even easier for the good government types to win, at least in some states. To start a movement, it might only take a few states to adopt the model laws. Of course, it would help if the first few were not negligible little states like Montana. Otherwise, the federal courts might brush them aside and say, "This or that 'model' law is preempted." Also, it would be best if there were a whole legislative program, put in place in six or seven states at least. Here's part of what could be in the program.

Put "Contract" Back in Employment Law

Go from tort back to contract. One model law should be: "Every employee of an employer is in an enforceable contractual relationship. No one may be fired except for just cause." The law should go on to require an individual written contract every year: "Every employee shall receive a contract setting out the employee's wage, health insurance, and benefits for the coming year. The contract shall contain the employee's vacation days and when the employee may take such vacation." This is not as radical as it may seem. I am not limiting the employer's right to change the terms of the contract from year to year, but forcing compliance for at least the coming year. Of course, I would go further. I think everyone should have a right under federal law to be in a union. But what I am proposing is just a *state* law, one that a right-wing federal court might not swoop in to preempt.

If an employee is fired and believes it is without just cause, then the employee may proceed in court. However, there should be mandatory arbitration, with a panel of state arbitrators. The arbitrations should be short. The losing party may appeal and obtain a jury trial or judge (at the appellant's option). But if the losing party does not prevail, it must pay the costs and legal fees of the other side.

The arbitrators need not, and should not, be state employees. I'd let the parties pick or have the state choose among a qualified panel of private-sector lawyers. (If my model law goes into effect, I'm thinking of applying, actually.)

If this is not your idea of contract, you can call it tort. But it's not like the civil rights law. It's not about the employer's subjective intent. There is no need to rifle through the e-mails of five to twenty people in middle management. We simply look at "fairness," in an objective or external way.

"Here's what he or she did. Is it fair to fire?"

Fairness might be a shock, a kind of political Big Bang.

More Trust Law

Yes, let's take the law of trusts, which needs a bit of perking up. In the case of hospitals, there is hope at this writing that they will be more accountable. Yes, things are improving—a little. But in the long run we need a model law for each type of charitable institution. Each has particular responsibilities. In Illinois the Attorney General is seeking to require charitable hospitals to give a certain percentage in "charity," or free care. This may sound crude, like physical French-type state planning, but that's exactly what the charities need. We cannot leave it up to the market to decide how much charity care a charity should give. In the same way there should be a certain percentage in "free tuition" and tuition caps for universities, including private charitable universities.

But let's assume that's too much. At least we can bar hospitals from suing the uninsured—or the uninsured at a certain income level or below. We can also require universities to pay the unpaid student loans when and if the student can show that the financial aid offered was inadequate or unreasonable in light of the university's charitable nonprofit status. Even if it is simply a case-by-case equitable standard, it is the kind of case judges have handled for centuries in the equity courts.

In addition, we should change the structure of the not-for-profits. At the very least, we should make them follow a kind of

Sarbanes-Oxley Act just for them. In the private sector, sections 302 and 906 of Sarbanes-Oxley require the chief executive officer and chief financial officer to certify that the books are honest. Not just "honest," but no misleading statements, nothing off the books, nothing cute—or else they go to jail. They have to certify, too, that they have a certain set of internal controls in place. They also have to pay for outside auditors who will rat on them if they are lying. These auditors do not work for them, but report to an outside independent board.

At the very least, some of the provisions in Sarbanes-Oxley could be adapted to apply to these charities, which are now run by corporate MBAs in much the way they run Microsoft or McDonald's. I mean that the officers of a charity should certify that they have made a good-faith effort to provide the maximum in charity, in terms of scholarships or free medical care or whatever. They should give honest numbers about the real charity and not try to pass off what is really bad debt. In addition, the charity should have to pay for the same type of outside independent auditor, who would report to the state and not to the charity itself as to how much "charity" the charity is actually giving, and require an audit of the charity application process. Is there adequate notice to all eligible? Are the standards being fairly applied?

And there could be criminal penalties, just as in Sarbanes-Oxley. There's no reason officers of a trust should be held to a lower standard of truth telling.

Employee Regulation, not Deregulation

There are other ways we can learn from Sarbanes-Oxley. And here I think we should say something good about the Bush administration: Sarbanes-Oxley is the greatest idea in regulation in our time, and it came under George W. Bush, of all people.

Of course he hates it. Indeed, the Republican Party hates it: it is regulation that is more far-reaching than even in social-democratic Europe. Our bankers now groan that Wall Street can't compete. If anyone says that nothing can change in this country, the short answer to that person is, "Look at Sarbanes-Oxley."

If it's so awful to the right, and if it's so loathed that the last and final irony is that liberal Democrats in the new Congress may be the ones repealing it, how did it ever go into effect? That's a good question—and the answer should give us hope: "They really had no choice."

Without a return to law, or without a turn away from deregulation, the new economy that the elite have been creating may turn out to be especially vulnerable to collapse. As my friend Richard Parker, who is an economic historian, says, "We actually are making or producing fewer and fewer things. How is it that we keep having so much more economic activity and growth, year after year? The answer is: 'People are making bets.' What we really have now is a 'faith-based' economy." More and more of our economic life depends on investors putting money into mutual funds, mortgages, futures, anything on which they can make a bet. And these bets depend on confidence, on trust. After World Com and Enron there was a moment when it seemed people might stop making bets. The danger to the betting was so great that even the right, in terror, slammed in Sarbanes-Oxley.

This didn't come from the New Deal. It didn't come from the left. It's true Sarbanes is a Democrat and it was his idea, but at the time it was only an idea. Our side had nothing to do with putting it into *law.*

And while the scare is now over, and the bets are on again, and the economy (the gambling part of it) is back on track and growing, and the CEOs are grumbling about Sarbanes-Oxley, and the Democrats in Congress may give in to them and try to ruin it, Sarbanes-Oxley or a "lite" version is probably here to stay. As the bets keep growing, investors need the safety, predictability, and the other virtuous things that we can get only from the Rule of Law.

They need some kind of legal system to come back.

But it has to be a new kind. They can't depend on the New Deal, which they can buy off. As I write, there is a new scandal of a Bush type blocking the SEC from pursuing a banker at Morgan Stanley. But it is not as easy to block Sarbanes-Oxley, because the regulation comes not from outside, from the government, but from inside—from the very structure of the firm. It is too much to say that it reinvents the corporation, but it changes the checks and balances from within.

Instead of regulating from the outside, we have installed a piece of software in the very gizzard of the corporation to make it a little less lawless, or even to behave. The CEO is forced to sign certain statements under penalty of perjury. Worse, the CEO has to pay out money for auditors who don't really work for him or her. Are they even part of the company? Yes, but after Sarbanes-Oxley, the concept of the company itself has changed.

In the same way that we have brought in outside auditors, we should bring in employees to enforce the law. Not by outside suits, as whistle-blowers, but directly, in a hands-on way, by participation within.

In Europe, or at least German-speaking Europe, this is routine: they have works councils. Employees make and enforce the rules. They don't need outside agencies of the state. And while I don't dream of putting in works councils here, we can take a certain baby step, in the spirit of Sarbanes-Oxley. Even a state like Montana could get out of the business of enforcing the state minimum wage or health and safety laws. Montana could pass a law: "Employees of Montana companies shall have the right to elect committees of employees to enforce applicable Montana employment laws."

In a way, think of it as an extension of Sarbanes-Oxley, with a set of hourly-worker auditors to see that the laws of Montana are being carried out. At the local Wal-Mart, people could even run for office, for it is an office of a certain kind. This is even more important than Sarbanes-Oxley because it gives people something to do. It creates opportunities to participate. "To my fellow employees at Wal-Mart! If elected, I promise to make sure there is no working off the clock." It gives people a chance they rarely have now in our country to make the law their own.

Institutionalize the Whistle-Blower

Or break up the state Attorney General's office into "a lawyer for the state" and an "ombudsman at large," separately elected. This is a way to stop the use of the whistle-blower and the unpredictable "private" enforcement of public law. Look at the conflict of interest of even an Eliot Spitzer when he was Attorney General for New York. There is a basic conflict in being a business-type lawyer for a behemoth like the state of New York and being a tribune of the people. He could sue an insurance company like Aetna or Allstate for fraud, but not the state department of insurance for allowing it. Often, it's the state agency that's worse. Or perhaps he couldn't go after a company at all because it is a particular state agency's turf. Anyway, Spitzer was rare in the way he balanced both roles. The way to institutionalize Spitzer is to break up the Attorney General's office into two offices: one to defend the state, and the other to sue the state and other lawbreakers as well.

Reenact the Common Law

By that I mean take the law that they teach in law school and put it in state statutes, with direct private rights of action. Put in the principles of corporate law, such as corporate waste, but make clear that "waste" can be a superbonus at Disney, or any supersalary when the company is failing. It is weird the number of states whose laws do not have the laws we learn in law school. Since a law against an excessive bonus is not in writing, judges lose the nerve to enforce it, even if they could do it under the so-called unwritten common law. It is easier to deregulate this older common law if it is never written down. Even when it is written down, it is a battle to get a judge to enforce it. Many lawyers I know have struggled to get judges to enforce the common-law fiduciary duties of ERISA, even though, in section 404 of ERISA, Congress expressly says there is a duty of "loyalty, prudence, skill, care." It's even easier for a court to let the duty go if it is not in a state law, in writing. The single best thing to bring security and stability to the Rule of Law would be to copy out the old law of corporations and the law of trusts and just put them in state statutes.

"Oh no, the common law should evolve. That's why it isn't in the state statutes." It isn't evolving. It's vanishing. Let's write it up before all of it is gone.

True, the for-profit corporations can go on incorporating in friendly states such as Delaware. Still, a set of model laws might change the legal climate of the courts even in states like Delaware.

Go into the Lending Business

What about usury? I have little hope that even a Democratic Congress would ever put in a national interest-rate cap. So should we give up? No. In a few states, there may be a chance to "charter" a state-funded bank with little "stores" that would lend out small bits of cash to people of good character. Let the bank charge 25 percent. But the bank could be choosy, as a bank used to be, and lend to the honest single mothers whom a Jimmy Stewart would have helped. As to the big banks, yes, they could keep their licenses to charge what they like. But every two years, a bank would have to ask the state to renew it. At this time, the bank would have to prove to the state that it still had a reputation for "honesty" and "fairness," as the old state laws used to require. The up-to-date twist is that a new consumer-rights agency could now weigh in on each bank's application. "Here's what that bank has been doing in our courts." Just the idea that anyone is watching these collection cases might have a chilling effect on the number of suits being filed against people like Ms. H.

This is part 1 of the program, and even this is in a partial version. It leaves out a lot. About releases, for example: let's prohibit them unless they are mutual, or have true mutuality. The poor employee or consumer has to represent: "This is knowing and voluntary." But the employer or business should also have to represent: "I declare I have provided all relevant facts." The employer or business should be subject to a penalty clause if this is not true.

There's more. Company arbitrations, interest rates—to set out all of this would take too long, and it would be tedious to a nonlawyer. Let's go on to part 2 of the program, the more important part: enforcing Footnote Four.

In the long run, we have to pass and enforce laws to which people give a real, and not a "notional," consent. We have to return to something like majority rule. Maybe some people fear a real democracy would lead to gridlock. Look at Europe, look at France, look at Germany: economists gasp. Since they have one person, one vote and majority rule, people can more easily resist deregulation. Aside from the laws being fairer, such countries are less volatile and more politically stable as a result.

If I were arguing with a conservative, I'd make a point of this stability. The case for a system with a Rule of Law and not one of continuous ad hoc deregulation is the stability that results. No one really rich is going to care about Rawls or the Original Position; no one can imagine being back in the womb. But I would try to get people to imagine the Ultimate Position: which set of arrangements increases the long-run likelihood that you will keep what you have got? Or let's put it more directly: which set of arrangements is more likely to survive, without undue instability, a three-year recession, or a drop in per capita consumption of 10 percent or so?

The answer is: a system or Rule of Law with real popular consent.

So that's the case for Footnote Four: not from the Original Position but the Ultimate Position. Not at any given moment, but in the long run, to the very end. That's what appeals to me about it—not just as a liberal but to the extent I'm a conservative. Without consent to limit them, the people who normally run things go too far to the right and get all of us in trouble. We have had a little taste of this with Bush.

Yes, the takeover of Congress by the Democrats, in 2006, has been a check. But the check should have come earlier, and it should have been much stronger. In the last election, absent gerrymandering, the Democrats could (and should) have won forty-five or more House seats instead of only twenty-seven.

In short, in this time of growing plutocracy at home and military defeat abroad, it's time to strengthen some of our constitutional arrangements. Being a lawyer, I tend to think in suits. I will list a few we need and some of the legislative fixes too.

Sue on Gerrymandering

Until now, as I noted, the two parties have controlled both sides of the lawsuits over gerrymandering. "Oh, what we do is okay, but what you do is too much." It's time for ordinary people to sue. Stop it, all of it. "But you can't stop it," people say. Sure you can. Iowa has done it. It has come up with a commission with two Democrats and two Republicans. To break a tie, they have a neutral.

In other words, sue to get a process, not a map. Courts hate to get into drawing maps. "Your Honor, our expert says the line should go down Maple Street over here, instead of Elm Street over there."

No. Stop asking the court to pick a map.

Instead of picking the map, make the state (Texas, Illinois) come up with a process that is free of politics. I mean, a map-drawing process that does not look at polling data or voting data to show how the parties will do. Is it possible? It's not only possible but it's the law in a handful of states. Make it the law of the land.

Then the House of Representatives can truly represent the people, not just on a freak basis, in case of a war, as in 2006, but reliably for the long term.

Deal on the Filibuster

In the long run, the bigger evil is the Senate. Alas, no court is going to toss out the whole Senate as such. "Draw a new map of the fifty states, with equal populations." No, that won't happen. But the Democrats could at least give up the filibuster.

Even when the Democrats were a Senate minority, one way

would have been to madden the GOP into zapping it: going nuclear, as they say. In July 2006, the Senate Republicans almost did zap the filibuster. The Democrats were holding up too many of Bush's judicial nominees. At the last minute, there was a compromise: the filibuster was "saved."

Why save it?

The Republicans would have done the left a favor. If there is no filibuster, there is a chance that in 2008, a labor law reform bill like the Employee Free Choice Act could pass the Senate. Suppose in 2008 there were a Democratic president *and* Senate *and* House. Then, if there were no filibuster, labor's bill might actually pass.

Right now, the Democrats could go nuclear and zap the filibuster, and nothing would happen. Since Bush can veto any labor law reform anyway, the GOP in the Senate might not be *that* upset. Gridlock would go on. The Fourth Republic, even without a filibuster, would be intact.

Why not zap it now, while there is no immediate painful effect on either political party? Or the Democrats could even be good sports about it: "We'll keep it for now, but not for 2008, since people are entitled to elect a Senate."

Besides, with no filibuster, Republicans may calculate Bush's nominees would have a chance if they could peel off a Joe Lieberman. Yes, did I think about that? I sure did, and it would be worth it even for a one-in-three chance that in a few years people would have a right to join a union.

Use Game Theory to Zap
the Electoral College

To my surprise, there already exists a group with the same idea. It's simple. Have each state pass a law that sends delegates to the Electoral College in the same ratio as the outcome of the state's popular vote for president. So if Maine voters pick Kerry

over Bush by 55 percent to 45 percent, then the electors go
to the Electoral College in the same ratio. No one wins the
"whole" vote. So far only Maine has such a procedure.

Other states hesitate. They hesitate because they figure they
will be even more ignored: "California is still delivering forty-
five votes to one candidate, but we're going to split our three
little dinky votes two to one. No way! We'll be even more negligible." Well, California is negligible now, since the Democrats have a lock on it. But to deal with this irrational concern,
the states could adopt this system, but hold off putting it into
effect until forty other states go along.

What about the others?

I think constitutional peer pressure will keep the other ten
states from holding out. I admit, it's based on the same belief
as Winston Churchill's—that in the end we Americans will
always do the right thing, after all the other alternatives
have been exhausted. Deep down, we're all sick of the Electoral College.

Get Rid of Voter Registration

Here there is a chance to do it by a lawsuit. How? A state has
to keep a list of people for jury duty. Typically, each county has
a jury commissioner. Until the 1990s, as I noted above, the
jury commissioner picked jurors from the voter registration
list. The problem? People stopped voting, but litigation kept
going up. Something had to give. The commissioners then
began to canvass everyone with a state photo ID.

And as it turns out, virtually everyone has a state photo ID.
Even the poor. Especially the poor. "They need it to cash their
checks at the Currency Exchange," a friend at the Legal Assistance Foundation said. In other words, a jury commissioner
can get a list of every person with a state photo ID and register
them.

If we can and should register everyone for jury duty, we can also register every voter by the *same process*. In some counties in Illinois there is a list that is more or less a list of every eligible voter, because everyone is needed for jury duty. In the 1970s, maybe in the 1980s, it was not so clear that the state could register everyone, more or less. But now it can.

Not only can the state register everyone; it has a constitutional duty to do so. While most states use driver's licenses to "supplement" their jury duty lists, they still go first to the voter registration lists. The states still use the lists disproportionately. To get out of jury duty, it is still rational not to register, and there is still a burden on the right to vote. It may be hard to notice in a big town like Chicago. Here, there are jurors aplenty. But in small counties, the registered voter is "on call" for jury duty for up to two weeks. Why?

There's no reason to sit there for two weeks reading *People* and watching *Oprah*. The state can put together a complete list of eligible citizens.

If the state has a duty to create such a list, then there is no constitutional justification for continuing the old system of voter registration. What would be the reason? It can't be fraud. A list based on photo IDs would be much better at preventing fraud. What other reason? It can't be expense. It's simpler to keep one list than to go on maintaining two, one for jury duty and one for voting.

Get rid of the second list, the old voter registration list: there is no rational administrative reason for it. To the contrary, only a single list makes sense. And if the old voter registration list is gone, we would not have to exclude nonregistered citizens from voting—that is, we would not have a rule barring what may be up to a third of adult U.S. citizens from voting on the day of the election.

Now, I doubt many of them will vote. But a few might pay attention, at the last minute, if the race is close. It would lead to a bit more majority rule. Besides, there is another change that we should make by lawsuit or statute.

Mail Everyone a Ballot

First, register them all to vote—all the people. Then, mail them all a ballot. Oregon mails a ballot to every registered voter, although Oregon does not register everyone to vote. Let's do both. And there is a good legal argument for requiring the mailing of a ballot.

The argument is: people have a right not just to vote, but to cast an informed or intelligent vote. It is not possible to do so by going to the polls and standing there and filling out the long U.S.-type ballot, which may have forty or more races. What is this, an exam? Even my friends accuse me: "You want it to be a take-home. You think there's a right to a take-home exam?" Yes, I surely do.

I'd hate to vote online. The technology isn't safe. But as I get to the bottom of the ballot, I'd like to be able to Google the candidates. In person, at the polling place, it's too late; I'm out of luck. "Who the heck are these guys?" You show up all proud of being a citizen, and you have to sneak away like a fool.

It's a culture of shame. "Heck, I can't even fill out a ballot."

No one can. So mail it. The Warren Court precedents are there for a right to an "informed" vote. We should bring a suit to get it.

Sue to Get Civics

Making it easier to vote is not enough. I'm aware of how mechanical and shallow points four and five will seem. They are, in a way. But they will up the turnout a bit, and in the polarized

United States, split evenly, it won't take much of an increase in lower-income votes to put an end to this divided, see-saw Fourth Republic. A stable majority is a precondition for any attempt to restore what I would call a stable Rule of Law.

But it's not enough—not in a country with as much civic disengagement as we have.

In the long run, it's not enough to make it easier to vote. We have to teach kids they have a moral obligation to vote. When Bush went into Iraq, my friend Jim Weinberg went to a few colleges and tried to do 1960s style teach-ins. He gave up. "They don't know anything." Also, they had no opinions. So he came to realize that he had to write off the colleges and start going into high schools. Teach them something, civics, current events—anything! Wake them up politically in this numbing world of No Child Left Behind.

Here's my idea: sue to require the same amount of civics in *all* the public schools in the way that only the very best college-prep type of public schools are permitted to teach. It's not just unfair. It's a denial of equal protection, or of an equal right to vote. In most states, a few elite public schools teach current events and problems of democracy. The others do not. But this is a disparate type of state assistance in the exercise of the right to vote. It's as if some kids are taken aside and told: "You're going to be the leaders." Other kids are told: "For you, there's no money for civics."

I admit, the better solution here is legislative. In every high school, why not require four years of civics? Some will gasp. Sure, this would be expensive. But it costs money to keep a republic. What about the standardized tests? Fine: let's test reading and comprehension. But let's turn them into civics tests. If we are serious about keeping our republic, we better rethink the whole concept of high school. If the vast majority still go no further than high school, then a high school degree in and of itself should pay off. One way: teach the kids to go out and vote. I mean, vote in a higher minimum wage, a bigger public pension. It may be an even better way than college to raise their standard of living.

Besides, they aren't going to college—so let's teach them to be citizens instead.

And it's not just in their self-interest, but in yours and mine as well. It's even in the interest of the rich, for without this consent to check and balance them, they may destroy themselves.

That's the Plan. Is it possible?

Epilogue

Maybe not! But I'm sick of these suits that go nowhere and leave people in a rage. I fear the suits will get even more spiteful or irrational as we deregulate our laws. In some cultures it is thought that such private litigation is a way of buying off or pacifying the malcontents. My friend S said this is supposed to be what they do in India: the people who are the natural troublemakers sue and get what they want, and that depoliticizes them.

But in our courts, the people who bring Title VII and other suits don't get what they want. They end up in a rage. And as we deregulate, we unintentionally stir up even more litigation than before. Once settled law is upended, we turn on each other and shout. Yes, the cases "settle." What people have lost—the loss of contract rights, pensions, or health insurance—will haunt them in the years to come. What they go through—in depositions, not in court but away from court, in private law offices—will only add insult to the injury.

So I'd like to bring back legal rights, and predictability, and order. It certainly wouldn't end lawsuits, but it might hold down the rage.

On top of it, it might even be a good thing for my country, too. As I write, we are in the middle of a war to put democracy in Iraq. It is now common to mock the neocon illusion that we could invade a country and slap in a democracy and go away.

Yes, it was an illusion. But if so, it was the mirror image of another illusion, one that people on the left have as well, that it does not take a lot of work to keep a democracy here. For us, after 1989, it is easy to take democracy for granted. It is "natural." It comes to us as easily as breathing. Look around the world: democracy is everywhere.

Indeed, there is no such thing anymore as American exceptionalism, since so many other countries have our kind of republic and our type of Rule of Law.

But it may turn out that it is harder for the United States to continue a democracy because it has a more antique and even an "un-republican" Constitution. Ours may have been the first modern democracy governed by the Rule of Law, but for that very reason, our priority in time, we could be the first to lose it all as well. So in a way, there is still a case for American exceptionalism: we have to work harder to keep a republic than people in other countries do.

The less we are a republic, the more unmoored we are from a stable Rule of Law. The more we deregulate—not just contract law, or trust law, but treaty law as well—the more trouble we seem to cause in the world. In the *Financial Times* the other day, I saw a poll of people in Europe, Canada, and Australia: a plurality pick the United States as the biggest danger or source of discord in the world. Of course, I disagree! But I can understand how this has happened. In an essay entitled "Universal Peace," Kant—the one the neocons love to mock—says that to the extent other countries become more republican in their constitutions, there will tend to be more international law. But there is a corollary as well: to the extent such countries become less republican in their constitutions, there will tend to be less international law, or it will be harder to sustain.

As we become less republican in our Constitution, we are predictably creating more trouble in the world. They want more law. We want less. The danger is that the less law we want, both at home and abroad, the worse will be our moral character. Here's the one thing that I grudgingly believe about the law. It's also something that has been put very well by Kant. He says that the very act of talking about law, or arguing over law, tends to improve people's moral character. Now, part of me is sceptical. "What? Look at these guys who make $800 an hour." And yet this is not entirely without truth. Look at the so-called liberals who are now up on the Court. If I include Kennedy as a fellow traveler, most of them started as people of the right. What happened is that they "grew." And just as this can happen to individuals, it can also happen with a whole institution, as in the case recently of the American Bar Association. I do think that there is something about the law, even the incessant use of the word itself, that makes us a little better morally. Woodrow Wilson used the word "law" to justify the way we went to war. FDR did the same. Bush never uses the word "law" at all, or very rarely. He uses the words "liberty" or "freedom," but he has an almost allergic aversion to the word "law." And because in the United States we keep talking about the law, the word goes on casting this spell on us, just as it cast its spell on Jefferson, and on Lincoln, and on people like the solid Republican politician Earl Warren, who locked up the Japanese in internment camps but ended up as a moral hero. We can deregulate away, and argue for "flexibility" or "efficiency" or some other word, but it's eerie that the law keeps this magic, this power to charm, this power to enchant.

The law, the law, the law—it's still this incantatory thing. If we think about and talk about and argue about law, then there is a little hope. If we just say the word "law," we are changed, we take on a role, as a people under the law, and almost helplessly we begin to act better, and be better, than who we were before.